GETTING ACQUIRED

GETTING ACQUIRED

HOW I BUILT AND SOLD MY SᴀᴀS STARTUP

ANDREW GAZDECKI

MICROACQUIRE
P U B L I S H I N G

Getting Acquired: How I Built and Sold My SaaS Startup

Hardcover ISBN: 978-1-5445-2289-0

Paperback ISBN: 978-1-5445-2288-3

eBook ISBN: 978-1-5445-2287-6

Audiobook ISBN: 978-1-5445-2410-8

I'd like to dedicate this book to my son, Julian Timothy Gazdecki. If you're reading this, I hope you'll believe me now when I say your dad was a cool guy! Seriously, though, I credit my success to an unshakable determination to give you and the rest of our family a better quality of life. Right now, you're just two years old, but nevertheless, I want to thank you for being an awesome little dude, and I can't wait to see how you change the world.

CONTENTS

INTRODUCTION

ON AUGUST 15, 2017, I got a surprise phone call that almost destroyed my company.

I was giving a product demonstration to a local restaurant with my VP of Customer Success, Rosa Romaine. The mobile app we created was going to help them grow their business, and we were all super excited.

Then my mobile phone rang. I excused myself and motioned for Rosa to continue. I looked down at my iPhone and saw it was Stephen, my VP of Product. He knew I was in a meeting, so why was he calling now?

"Andrew," he said, his voice cracking. "I just got a call from one of our largest partners."

"What happened?" I asked.

"All their apps are gone."

"What do you mean, *gone?*"

"The App Store cleared them out."

I closed my eyes, balled my free hand into a fist, and sighed.

It's all over, I thought.

Since launching Bizness Apps in my dorm room in 2010, I'd been helping small businesses compete with megabrands through app-based marketing. Our app builder saved companies up to $100,000 on app development and helped them compete against bigger brands with even bigger pockets. It was David versus Goliath, and our software was the slingshot.

Only it seemed Goliath also had a trick or two up his sleeve.

The next four weeks after Stephen's phone call were a struggle for survival. Revenue fell 10 percent. Our best clients asked questions I couldn't answer. I still remember the sleepless nights, skipped meals, and permanent headache.

I spent most of my time on the phone with the Apple executive team, begging for a lifeline. I needed a response to an appeal on paragraph 4.2.6 in Apple's Developer Guidelines: *Apps created from a commercialized template or app generation service will be rejected.*

Paragraph 4.2.6 changed my industry forever. To Apple, it was just quality assurance. No clones, no sloppy code, no spam. But to ban *all* app builders? To us, it felt heavy-handed.

Nevertheless, my hands were tied. I was going to lose my company. Revenue was in freefall. Clients were asking for their money back. I dreaded resignation letters, the inevitable knocks on my door as employees fled the sinking ship. At my nadir, I remember laughing—yes, actually laughing—at how quickly my world had turned upside down. It was so sudden. It seemed so *inevitable.*

And then, a little over a year later, it flipped again.

On May 6, 2018, I sold Bizness Apps to ESW Capital, a $10 billion private equity firm, for a life-changing amount of money. I'd been a broke, twenty-something entrepreneur, fighting for the survival of my company, and now I had tens of millions of dollars in my account. I felt like the luckiest man alive.

The money was incredible. It felt like freedom. But when the shock wore off, I recognized a deeper sense of achievement.

I had hundreds of employees, and our apps served millions of people. I had changed the world and helped shape lives and livelihoods. And this, more than the money, is what hooked me on entrepreneurship.

Looking back, I could've given up countless times, so why did I keep pushing on? Why did I stay up until midnight answering customer support questions? Why would I wake up at three in the morning to help with server issues? And why did I push on after the Apple 4.2.6 debacle threatened to raze my business to the ground?

It's funny what the first acquisition does to you. It reveals things about yourself you might never have known. I don't really care for money or material things (apart from maybe one nice car), but I love helping people. I love having a purpose, a mission, a chance to impose order on a chaotic and unfair world. I kept going because I *love* what I do.

Today, with two acquisitions under my belt, I'm starting to think of the future. I can't wait to settle down, spend more time with my wife Michelle, and raise children. I want to be the father I never had. I want to see the look in their eyes when I tell them that in my early twenties I was running a multimillion-dollar software company featured in every magazine you can think of.

But my journey isn't over yet.

Now, I want to help entrepreneurs like you achieve the success I did. Perhaps more. There's a pattern to it—not a magic formula but a structure, a blueprint for boosting your chances of success. I know because I used it at Bizness Apps.

I used it again at my second acquired company, Altcoin.io, as a growth consultant for several multimillion-dollar start-ups, and I use it now as founder of MicroAcquire, a startup acquisition marketplace.

As I wrangled with Apple's 4.2.6 rejection, I reflected on my life as if it, too, was about to end. Yes, I know how absurd that sounds. Call it immaturity, if you like, but I'd invested so much of my time and effort into Bizness Apps that I believed I'd never recover if it failed.

Since I was a kid, I've always challenged the status quo. At twelve years old, I was interviewed by NBC, Fox News, the *LA Times*, and even *The Dr. Laura Program* for petitioning my local school to let me skateboard to campus. It was a fluff piece, I know, but that experience—that *failure*—is a lesson that stayed with me. About twenty years later, there I was again, up against a higher authority, Apple, standing in the way of change. I had to believe there was a way out. Otherwise, what was the point?

I *did* find the way out. And if you read on, you'll also find out how I tackled a myriad of other problems along the path to my first multimillion-dollar acquisition.

You'll discover how I got my companies featured in *TechCrunch* over a dozen times, how I became an *Inc.* fastest-growing company two years in a row (numbers fifty-eight and ninety-two), and how I finally achieved my dream of selling my startup for millions of dollars.

Not only that, but you'll learn how to build a compelling brand story and catalyze growth on a budget, and how to position, manage, and get the best out of an acquisition.

I'm Andrew Gazdecki, founder, mentor, and entrepreneur. I want to share my experiences with you so you can put into practice the lessons I learned without making the same mistakes. If you dream of starting, growing, and then selling your own business, you've come to the right place.

So grab a coffee, settle down, and let me tell you my story.

CHAPTER 1

PLEASE DON'T
GIVE ME A JOB!

HOW MANY BUSINESS BOOKS HAVE YOU READ? If you're anything like me, you've probably read hundreds. And while I've learned a lot from them, I still believe there's no better teacher than experience. I know that's a cliche, but like all cliches, there's a kernel of truth to it to which we've long become desensitized.

Think of when you learned to ride a bike. No one told you how to balance. No one taught you how to pedal. You picked it up through experience (and countless skinned knees). It's one thing being *told* what to do; it's another to learn the right way yourself.

You might be wondering, then, why I bothered to write this book. If I'm such a believer in learning through experience, learning by *doing*, why take the time and effort to distill what I've learned into these modest pages?

In many respects, what follows is typical of many business books. You'll read advice, tips, and strategies for building and selling profitable startups. But you'll also get an honest account of my experience as a serial entrepreneur: from being a penniless student on financial aid to selling my first business for millions of dollars.

You'll cringe at my mistakes, cheer the lessons I learned from them, and ride the roller coaster of emotions that is Startupland. You'll get to know me somewhat intimately, and I hope you will, through a kind of literary osmosis, live through my experiences and absorb these lessons as if they were your own.

I don't want you to make the same mistakes I did. At the same time, I don't want your ideas to stagnate until they fossilize. This book will show you that no matter who you are, where you're from, or what you do, you can build and sell profitable startups.

What follows is skewed toward Software-as-a-Service (SaaS). She was the first ship I sailed, and I haven't left her since. However, most principles apply to any industry, niche, service, or product. And you don't need a big chunk of capital to get started. In my experience, a startup needs to do just three things to be successful:

1. Solve a problem or fulfill a need or want.

2. Develop a viable business model.

3. Tell a great story.

You might have one nailed. Possibly two. Without all three, however, you'll never scale. You might make a bit of money (like I did when I was building apps for every small business in my college town), but you won't get much further than that. And that's fine. We *should* celebrate achievements, no matter the size. But if you had the opportunity to break into the big leagues, wouldn't you grasp it with both hands?

THE SPARK

Today, a lot of people ask me how Bizness Apps began. I could point to a hundred different moments: my past successes and failures, PhoneFreelancer (I'll talk more about this soon), my wife Michelle's support, my family and friends, the people who taught and mentored me over the years—I could go on. Without those lessons, that experience, the advice of people wiser than I'll ever be, I might never have spotted the opportunity that later became Bizness Apps.

To start, you might be surprised to learn I'm no coder. I'm not a savant or a math wiz, or even particularly academic. What I *am* is persistent. Bizness Apps wasn't my first rodeo as an entrepreneur. I'd been starting companies every summer since I was a teenager. While my friends were out surfing, playing sports, and hanging out at the skatepark, I was indoors squinting at my computer, brainstorming new business ideas.

I like to think most of my ideas were pretty good. One of my earliest came from the massively popular online multiplayer role-playing game *World of Warcraft* (*WoW*). The in-game economy runs on digital gold, which you buy using real money. If you want a fast track to the best weapons, armor, or magical items, you open your wallet and buy them from the auction market. That might sound nuts, but it made Blizzard, *WoW's* creator, billions of dollars. Never underestimate the power of escapism, people. And all this virtual cash got me thinking, *What if I could help these digital gold retailers find customers?*

Back in 2008, Google Ads were super cheap to run. So I created a website to pull buyers in and then redirect them to the retailer, earning an affiliate commission on every sale. Unfortunately, my gold-hawking scheme didn't last. Out of nowhere, Google Ads went from twenty cents a click to several dollars, pricing me out of the market. Needless to say, I didn't stay in the virtual gold business for long, but at its height I was making around $2,500 per month. Not bad for a nineteen-year-old, right?

Well, we all have to start somewhere. In late 2007, while studying at CSU Chico State, I built a job board called PhoneFreelancer. Back then, I was dirt poor. I lived on instant ramen and 7-Eleven coffee, wore my high school wardrobe, and partied on the cheapest, nastiest vodka ($1-a-drink cheap). That said, I've never been a flashy guy. The shirt I'm wearing now cost just $5 and all alcohol tastes the same to me, so I don't remember those years being especially hard. I was healthy, and as long as I was working to secure a comfortable future for my family, I was happy.

However, being broke meant little seed money for new ideas. As you know, I'm no software engineer, so I had to buy something ready-made that I could modify with a few simple lines of code. PhoneFreelancer began as a script: a prebuilt, customizable version of a website that I bought for a few hundred dollars. All it did was let people post and respond to job ads (much like Upwork), but I dedicated it to mobile app development. Businesses posted app ideas, and developers quoted to build them. I'd then get a 5 percent commission on the hire.

After launching PhoneFreelancer, I spent every waking second searching forums, blogs, and websites related to mobile app development. I stalked comment sections, harvested email addresses, and infiltrated message boards with a single goal: to promote my mobile app jobs board. While my peers had fled campus for summer vacations and internships, my summer job was promoting PhoneFreelancer. And I loved it.

If I'd been doing this as an intern at another company, I'd have been bored out of my mind. It was tedious and repetitive, and it bore few results. But this was *my* business. I'd have been just as happy mopping chum at a fish market had I been my own boss. That's the thing about entrepreneurship: you don't mind pulling your sleeves up and getting stuck into the grind.

Eventually, it paid off. Around three months after launch, people took notice. Sign-ups tripled in the space of a few weeks. At first, I couldn't believe it, but then I looked around me. There wasn't "an app for everything" quite yet, but momentum was building. Here was a new medium through which businesses could communicate with customers, and mobile apps were the gateway.

Years later, a change in Apple's developer guidelines would play a villain in the Bizness Apps story. But back in 2009, the App Store was a cash cow ready for some serious milking. People threw their money at Apple, and businesses threw their budgets into mobile-app development. Suddenly, the PhoneFreelancer job board was awash with app requests that developers were only too happy to fulfill. They raked it in, and so did I. At its height, PhoneFreelancer generated around $5,000 per month—a fortune to a broke college student. And things were about to get even more interesting.

In July 2009, a man called Vladimir emailed me with an offer to buy PhoneFreelancer. I never met Vladimir, but he owned a development agency. I remember seeing "$100,000" on-screen and blinking in disbelief. It was more money than I'd ever dreamed of having at that age. I must've read that email twenty times before the implications of it sunk in. I was young then, just twenty years old. I'd grown up in a consumer society without the means to consume. With a potential $100,000 in the bank, my mind ran wild. As I said, I've never been flashy, but never having money, this felt like my biggest achievement. It *was* my biggest achievement—until then, at least.

But I had an even bigger reason to sell. Something far more valuable than the money on the table. The best businesses often start with an observation of the world, of people and their behavior, and I noticed that PhoneFreelancer's customers were posting the same jobs over and over again. Restaurants, for example, wanted an app with menus, coupons, contact details, and table reservations. Basic stuff, really, but it was a developer's market. Businesses paid anything from $50,000 to $100,000, sometimes more, for a custom-built mobile application. It didn't matter that developers were building the same things over and over again and just slapping a new skin on top.

I thought, *What if I built and sold a template for the most common apps?* Once basic functionality had been built, all I needed to do was swap out screens, change fonts, add logos, and so on. If I used a recurring revenue model (charged a subscription fee), I could make apps affordable for even the smallest businesses at a fraction of the price of their next-cheapest alternative. I kept thinking, *Why isn't anyone doing this already?* This wasn't a gap in the market but a deep, yawning chasm that no one, to my knowledge, had noticed yet.

This eureka moment couldn't have come at a better time. With an offer of $100,000 on the table, it was like the universe was saying, "Build Bizness Apps already!" It was my first experience of what would later become a personal mantra: *celebrate small achievements.* You never know what's around the corner. Getting out while the going is good is what makes great entrepreneurs (more on this to come).

TRUSTING YOUR INSTINCTS

I knew I had a good idea, but I didn't know how good. With that money, I could hire someone to help develop a prototype, build the website, and then start selling these apps to local businesses: restaurants, gyms, hotels, shops, garages, bowling alleys, and so on. I was dazzled, intoxicated with its endless applications. Or maybe it was just the money. Looking back, I think it was both. I wanted the money, but I needed a reason to let go of PhoneFreelancer. The only excuse I could tolerate was seeding another business.

So I accepted Vladimir's offer, and the money landed in my account. What a strange moment that was. I guess some twenty-year-olds would've gone on a wild spending spree, but I didn't know what to do with it. My friends call me Simple Gaz. I'm about as ostentatious as oatmeal. But I did treat myself to a watch, a Nixon 51-30, which I bought for about $500 (a fortune to me at the time). I also took a lot of friends for nights out. For the first time in my life, I had money. Real money. What good was it if I didn't share it with the people I loved?

But as graduation loomed, I started to panic. The money hadn't run out, but I'd yet to do anything serious with it. As my friends applied for graduate schemes and entry-level positions, I dreaded the jobscape. To me, it was all office politics, slippery career ladders, and miserable managers forcing you into rigid roles. It signaled the death of autonomy, of giving up to a higher power. It reeked of the sort of helplessness I felt at school, of not having a say in my own future.

Of course, I'm not against working for other people. It's just not for me. So while my friends celebrated interviews at investment banks, insurance companies, and advertising agencies, I dug out my notes and prepared a plan to get Bizness Apps off the ground. At that time, I hadn't gone all-in on the template idea yet. I needed $10,000 to build the prototype, which was a big chunk of the remaining money from the sale of PhoneFreelancer after taxes. It was a risk, but if I could get enough local businesses to sign up, I could pay rent and maybe focus on building other startups.

Michelle, my then-girlfriend and now wife, was a little apprehensive at first. She'd always been my biggest cheerleader, and while Bizness Apps sounded great on paper, shelling out $10,000 for a prototype was a big step. I'd never spent that much on *anything*, never mind an idea, that, to my knowledge, no one had tried before. I mean, let's face it: what were the chances of *any* college kid making it with a $10,000 investment? I had zero work experience, zero managerial experience, zero sales experience, zero marketing experience, and zero coding skills. I'd learned entrepreneurialism on the fly, making hundreds if not thousands of mistakes, big and small, along the way. (How else do you learn?)

"Are you sure about this?" Michelle said one night after dinner. "It's a lot of money. Wouldn't you rather pay off your student loans first?" I could see the sense in her suggestion. To Michelle, it was a gamble, but to me, it was entrepreneurship. If I failed, I'd start again, stronger than before. But if I'd spent the money repaying loans I could easily defer, I wouldn't have gotten Bizness Apps off the ground until much later—perhaps too late to achieve the momentum needed for it to become a multimillion-dollar company.

After some debate, Michelle relented. In many ways, she was the secret co-founder of Bizness Apps. She grew up in a household of wise financiers who gifted stock to each other at Christmas, so she knew a thing or two about making (and saving) money. Often, when I was spinning plates, trying to do a million things at once, Michelle was the voice of reason. She helped me focus on the right things, and for that I'm forever grateful.

With Michelle on my side, I blazed ahead with the prototype, and let me tell you, it was a *mess*. I'd only partially grasped the concept, so the spec sheet was short and assumptive. The UI was ugly and lacked features. I could edit pictures and text but little else. Nevertheless, it was enough to start selling to small businesses. You could call it the Bizness Apps minimum viable product (MVP). Next was a "launch strategy," which is really just a fancy term for cold calling every restaurant and small business in the area.

Have you ever cold called before? I won't lie. It sucks. Of all the sales techniques, it's one of the least enjoyable. You spend most of your time charming your way past gatekeepers instead of talking about your product. I knew Bizness Apps could help small businesses grow and compete with larger businesses—I just needed to get it in front of people's eyes. But when you're the tenth caller that day, the gatekeeper's patience wears thin. You'd better have a polished elevator pitch, or you're going to crash and burn like I did many, many times. How did you explain the value of an app to a small-town restaurant before mobile marketing was a thing?

I remember asking a restaurant owner if they'd considered app-based marketing, and their reply was, "App? What's that? Like, appetizers?" It was a different time.

In the end, the less I spoke about the technology and more about what it could do—the couponing, interactive menus, happy hour promotions, and other means of drawing in new customers—the more demos I booked. I didn't charge tens of thousands of dollars or need months of coding. For a small monthly fee, I delivered a mobile app for any business on any budget. When I explained their national competitors were stealing market share with apps costing up to $100,000, they realized the chance of competing at a fraction of the cost was almost too good to be true.

My first customer was Ben Daters, the marketing manager of the gym at Chico State. Ben and I weren't close friends at the time, but I knew him well enough to ask if he'd be interested in a mobile marketing demonstration. I arrived at reception with a buggy, pre-release version of the app installed on my iPhone. As I tapped away through the demo, avoiding broken buttons, Ben asked the right questions. He was one of the first to see the value in a presence on the App Store, probably because he was surrounded by fit young people sporting iPhones like fashion accessories. He signed up that day, and I remember going back for a workout a few weeks later to see the app advertised on the gym's TVs. *I made that!* I thought, smiling. Ben and I have been friends ever since.

Again, I rejected the frat parties and beer pong in favor of the dull blue glare of my laptop screen. I built the Bizness Apps website and collected contact information of local businesses. Then I started calling them to arrange meetings and product demos. Had I been doing this for anyone else but myself, I'd have been slacking off to join my friends at the bar. I can't overstate how important it is to love what you do. Otherwise, what's the point? You end up slaving away with no sense of purpose or achievement. You don't always have to *enjoy* it, but you must love it all the same. When you love something, you embrace it, warts and all, which is how I survived those first few months of Bizness Apps without throwing my phone at the wall!

THE TURNING POINT

Chico was the perfect launchpad for Bizness Apps. It was a college town with a thriving student-driven economy. Local businesses were fighting to connect with students, and what better way than through this hip, new technology in everyone's palm? By the time I had ten customers, I was raving about Bizness Apps to anyone who'd listen. "This is gonna be a million-dollar company," I'd tell my friends. They'd look at me in my faded jeans, high-school Vans, and ten-dollar haircut and think I was crazy.

That all changed at the 2010 CSU Chico State Entrepreneurial Contest. I'd entered this competition the previous three years, winning, fourth, third, and second place, respectively, with PhoneFreelancer. I both loved and hated it. Each year I didn't win first place was like a slap in the face. I was cocky, sure, but most of the winners would've needed millions of dollars just to get off the ground, where I'd always started my businesses with next to nothing. So it had felt, in some ways, a bit elitist.

Bizness Apps was already a profitable business when I entered it into the competition. My cold-calling scheme had worked. I'd acquired around seventy customers and was generating around $2,000 to $3,000 per month in revenue ($39 per month per customer). Every business at Chico State used an app I'd built, but I wanted more. I wanted to reach a thousand customers and beyond, and I couldn't do this alone. I knew the judging panel was composed of local business owners and teachers, some of whom would have the contacts to turn Bizness Apps from a profitable side project into a high-growth, fully fledged startup.

On the one hand, the competition was about validating my hard work. I was barely out of my teens and had built this cool business from my dorm room. I wanted approval from my mentors and peers. But on the other hand, it was also an investor pitch. If I could convince these people of Bizness Apps' potential, I might also find someone to help take it to the next level. You'd think this would have made me nervous, but having seen the competing entries, I wasn't worried. Forgive my slightly cocky tone here, but honestly, none of them had legs. I remember one being a tracking chip for babies—because babies are known for their quick getaways, right?

The contest works like this: first, you give a presentation, and then afterward there's a Q&A session with the judging panel. The presentation is the easy part. With enough preparation, I'd sail through it as I had done in previous years. But the grilling afterward was always scary. You just never knew what they'd ask you. You'd get the usual stuff like, "How are you going to scale?" "How will you take this to market?" "How will you find new customers?" and so on. But there were always curveballs, and to be frank, I wasn't sure how I'd answer the others either.

Until then, I'd acquired all my customers through cold calling and referrals. It was a dependable but slow strategy, and not nearly smart enough to scale the business before anyone else replicated my formula. As soon as my first customers rolled in, it was only a matter of time before someone copied my business model, perhaps even improving it. I was in a race to scale and had enjoyed a head start so far. But if I didn't grow fast enough, I'd be a small-town business forever, and I had much bigger ambitions than that.

I remember the quiet murmur of the audience as I took to the auditorium stage, the lights bright and hot, the row of judges shuffling papers and jotting down notes. My hands were shaking, but more from excitement than nerves. I'd practiced this presentation fifty times. I was ready.

"Good afternoon, ladies and gentlemen," I said. "Today, I'm going to show you how to build a mobile app in just five minutes."

Over the next few minutes, I built an app for the contest, including a list of contestants and their submissions and a feedback form. I even sent a push notification to my mobile phone saying, "Andrew Gazdecki is definitely going to win this competition," and showed it to the audience (I told you I was a bit cocky). Then came Bizness Apps' revenue chart, customer chart, and usage statistics. "Any questions?" I asked at the end.

I'll never forget the look on the judges' faces. They were incredulous, staring bug-eyed and open-mouthed, as if I'd just revealed the secret of cold fusion, not a versatile mobile-app builder. I'd imagined this moment a thousand times but never expected it to come true. None of the judges had any questions. I'd stunned them into silence, and it was the proudest moment of my life. I think what struck them most was my viable business model with enormous potential. But I'd yet to prove how well it could scale, and this is what I would focus on next.

One of my mentors and favorite teachers, Peter Strauss, pulled me aside after the contest. He was the Head of the Entrepreneurship Department (now retired) and he'd helped me with other businesses before, including PhoneFreelancer. "Andrew," he said. "You really impressed me today. I always knew you had potential, but today, you surpassed it. Well done." Those words meant more to me than all the revenue in the world. My business had been validated by one of the most esteemed entrepreneurs in the state.

At this point, I'd already been working on Bizness Apps for months. Maybe, in an alternate timeline, it would still have become what it is today. But I like to think the point at which the company crystallized and took on a momentum of its own was when it won that contest.

I was still high on the win, reveling in the possibilities opening up before me, when Peter said, "I'd like you to meet a friend of mine." This friend, Christian Friedland, a loud, brash entrepreneur with a penchant for flashy cars and sports coats (my opposite in every way) would help build Bizness Apps into the force of change it is today.

I was still the rookie—young, naive, and swinging for the fences. Christian Friedland, on the other hand, was the heavy hitter; an older, wiser, seasoned player. Together, we'd put our mobile apps in the hands of millions of people around the globe. But first, we had to solve the scalability problem. How could we grow Bizness Apps from a small-town project into a global phenomenon before anyone else caught up?

CHAPTER 2

CHICO

Time to Get Serious

WHEN I FIRST MET CHRISTIAN FRIEDLAND, I was a little starstruck. He was one of the richest people at Chico State, and I'd attended a number of his entrepreneurship seminars. I'd learned a lot from the guy, so I was really excited to meet him.

Peter Strauss had given Christian my number, and he called a few days after the contest, congratulating me on winning first place and suggesting we meet for dinner at Tres Hombres, a restaurant I'd built an app for some time earlier.

I was the first to arrive, and the waiter sat me at a table by the window. I was nervous and thirsty, and I ordered some water. I had no idea what the meeting would be about. I assumed Christian had some advice to share or maybe some contacts interested in becoming Bizness Apps customers.

About five minutes after I arrived, Christian pulled up in a gleaming black Mercedes CL500. He stepped out in polished brogues, chinos, and a fitted sports jacket—every bit the extravagant entrepreneur I'd known him to be. I suddenly felt my age and inexperience and was terrified of saying something stupid.

After a warm, strong handshake, Christian sat down.

"You want a drink?" he asked.

"Water's good," I said, wanting to stay sharp.

Christian turned to the waiter and asked to see the menu. "I'll have the burrito combo and a Cuba Libre. Thanks."

The waiter left, and Christian steepled his fingers together. I smiled, and for a moment I thought he was waiting for me to say something.

"How many customers do you have?" he asked.

"Seventy. Including this one," I said and handed over my iPhone.

I walked him through the Tres Hombres menu and loyalty system, answering his questions along the way. I'd delivered hundreds of these demonstrations, so it didn't feel like an interview.

Christian's questions were insightful and got me thinking about the future. He was especially interested in how adaptable the template was, what its limits were, how it might be improved, and so on.

Then he said something that almost made me spit out the water I'd been sipping.

"I'll give you $25,000 for 10 percent of your company."

I froze. Of all the possible reasons for this meeting, I'd never expected an offer of investment. And certainly not within the first thirty minutes of meeting him. I had no LLC, no corporation—it was just me. A kid with a website.

"I'm not sure," I said, trying to sound confident. "I don't really know you that well. Give me a week to think about it. Let me show you some more stuff, and then we can meet again. I'll bring a pitch deck."

The next day, Christian emailed me a profit and loss statement to complete. He needed to know how many customers I had at $39 per month in month one, month two, and so on. He also needed other data that would indicate the strength and potential of Bizness Apps, which, at the time, had yet to venture further than Chico's borders. I'd never done a P&L statement before, so it took a while to figure out the numbers. And more than that, I didn't want to mess it up and embarrass myself.

We had a meeting booked for the following week. As I completed the P&L, I had this bundle of nervous energy inside me. Christian was a proven entrepreneur, a known angel investor. He'd built and sold his business, Build.com, for $50 million, which continued to grow long after he walked away. This put him on a plane well above my own. Besides, I was sure that the first meeting hadn't been an introduction. He'd been feeling me out, testing me. The next meeting, I suspected, would be much harder.

So as I sat on the bus on the way to Christian's offices, I felt like I was leaving something behind. An younger self, I guess.

What happened next would determine the next phase of my life, and as I watched the sunlit streets of Chico roll by, leaves skittering along the sidewalk, it was a bittersweet moment. I wanted to capture everything—the nerves, the people on the bus, the fall colors swirling outside the window—and freeze it forever in my mind. If the meeting went well, my life would never be the same again.

"What do you *want*, Andrew?" Christian asked fifteen minutes into my pitch.

I'd been walking through the mechanics of the template, but it seemed Christian had made up his mind before I'd even walked through the door.

Another investor, Robert Strazzarino, a serial entrepreneur who'd invested in several successful SaaS businesses, was at the meeting. I later learned he had also founded one of his most profitable businesses, College Scheduler LLC (which was later acquired), while still a sophomore at California State University. If I'd been looking for a good omen, Robert was it.

"I want $50,000 for 10 percent," I said, meeting Christian's eyes.

Christian nodded, ruminating, and then he and Robert exchanged glances.

"15 percent, and we do the deal right now."

My palms began to sweat. I glimpsed a future of endless rounds of fundraising, losing my company one piece at a time. If I gave in now, when everything was in play, what kind of founder would I be?

"Sorry, Christian," I said. "I can't let you win this one. If you want to do $50,000 for 10 percent, then we have a deal." They stood up from their chairs, smiling. It had been gentle sparring, only natural among businesspeople of their caliber. They were happy. I was happy. We shook hands, and the deal was done. But as smooth as the negotiation was, that feeling of losing a chunk of what I'd worked so hard to build would stick with me for years. If I let others buy control of my company, I'd have less say in how it was run and might as well have gotten a job working for someone else. And that, dear reader, was the last thing in the world I wanted, and for a good reason, as you'll read in the following chapters.

I walked out of Christian's offices with a check in my hands for $50,000 payable to Bizness Apps LLC. I couldn't even bank it yet, but I didn't care. The investment was far more than money. It was a golden ticket out of the job market and into the startup business. Bizness Apps had been sanctioned, approved, *affirmed*. I was leaving college to run my own business—no bosses, no rules, no grinding away to line someone else's pockets. I was about to become CEO of my very first LLC, and I couldn't have been more excited.

Fifty grand is modest compared to what most startups raise, but for me, a solo nontechnical founder, it was a fortune. I could've squandered it all on swanky offices and a PA, burning it all in the first few months, but thankfully, that stuff never interested me. Bizness Apps HQ was a modest room, costing just $400 a month. It was little more than a box, really—maybe three times the size of my dorm room at

Chico State. But it was mine. I remember skating to work that first morning, warm breeze through my hair, sun on my cheeks, board clacking along the pavement, thinking, *This is it. I've done it. I'm living my dream.*

You might think that was a little naive, but I was desperate to avoid employment, not because I was lazy or unambitious but because it represented confinement—a place where dreams went to die. To me, the workplace was like school, somewhere I'd be forced to do others' bidding. But there I was, skating to work, doing what my teachers had denied me: experiencing true freedom for the first time in my life. What's more, I'd *earned* that freedom. I wasn't some dumb rich kid playing with daddy's money. I was a broke twenty-one-year-old student betting everything on an idea that I could change the world if I had the space to do it.

That said, I was still a kid. I went out drinking every weekend. I failed my entrepreneurship classes. I even redid my final year at Chico State so I could claim financial aid to pay my rent. I was hustling back then, with little idea of what it meant to be CEO. And I wasn't completely free, either. I had to ensure Christian and Robert earned a return on their investment, or I'd lose their respect. They were role models, and I couldn't bear to disappoint them.

GEARING UP FOR THE CHALLENGES AHEAD

My first official task as CEO was to hire some help. I had no distribution strategy at that stage, just a mobile phone and a business directory. If I wanted growth, I needed a workforce. I convinced two of my college friends, Zach Cusimano and Stephen Heisserer, to join me. They were cool guys, charming and enthusiastic about the project, but I don't think either of them considered the job a serious career move at the time. We were just a group of friends hanging out, making calls, and laughing together, learning as we went. We worked hard, and steadily our customer acquisition numbers rose.

In 2008, about a year after the Apple App Store debuted, Google launched Google Play. Until then, we'd made iOS apps exclusively. We were locked into the Apple ecosystem, but now there were Apple people and Android people. Apple had the lion's share of the market but was losing ground as people switched sides. Manufacturers like Microsoft, Nokia, and Samsung started adding features Apple didn't have, and for a cheaper price. As Android phones proliferated, we realized Bizness Apps *had* to be multiplatform. We had to be where the people were, and that meant releasing an Android version of Bizness Apps. We even considered building BlackBerry apps since the phones were still very popular back then, but thankfully we didn't—a smart move considering BlackBerry all but died a few years later.

Android was a huge deal for us, an untapped market with enormous potential. I was super excited about it, more so than the iOS launch. Back when I launched Bizness Apps, I was hustling from my dorm room, surrounded by empty pizza boxes and cans of Red Bull. I hadn't met Christian yet, hadn't won the Entrepreneurial Contest at Chico state, and had no idea if Bizness Apps would even get off the ground. But now I had investors, a company, and the support of my peers and mentors. Most of all, I had a great product that had shed its bugs and was ready for mass consumption. So why not turn the Android launch into the iOS launch we never had?

I applied to present the Android version of Bizness Apps at the 2010 DEMO conference in San Jose. Why DEMO? If you're working in SaaS or technology in general, you can't find a better platform from which to launch your product or service. The conference is bustling with journalists and entrepreneurs looking for a sneak peek at the next big thing. If accepted, you get to present your product to the entire conference. There's an incubator feel to the whole thing. The conference fosters innovation while mentoring founders, which is motivating when you're young and just beginning your entrepreneurial career. Blow them away at DEMO, and that's permission to go forth and conquer.

I just couldn't shake the disbelief when we got the acceptance call. My friends and I were in the office nursing bad hangovers, and we just looked at each other and laughed. We were three college kids playing startup, and now we were going to present at one of the most prestigious tech events of the year. Best hangover cure ever. You'd think that would've had us shooting straight until the conference, but our hubris had us partying right up until the night before. We drove to San Jose and had to stop a few times so I could be sick. That's how short-sighted I was back then. Everything was dreamy and unreal, and I guess I was a little intoxicated by it all.

We arrived at this awful hotel in San Jose. You know the type: frayed carpets, peeling wallpaper, and the smell of old newspapers and cigarettes. No Hilton or Marriott suite for us. Not even separate rooms. Even with the money rolling in from subscriptions, I had a tight hold on the purse strings. We spent as little as possible, thinking that the more we grew, the more permission we'd have to spend, which was just good financial sense. Instead of paying for some upmarket hotel or three separate rooms, we dropped our suitcases inside a musty old box with just two single beds. "You guys take the beds," I said. "I'm cool with the floor." So the night before one of the biggest presentations of my life, I slept on a floor like a drunken frat boy without a care in the world.

We arrived at DEMO the next morning and set up the Bizness Apps booth. Many of the attendees were investors looking for the next big thing, and while we weren't looking for investment, per se, we did want to shake the foundations a bit. As three college kids, we were optimistic and enthusiastic. We had a product with huge potential, and our energy attracted a decent crowd. We collared everyone as they walked past to show Bizness Apps in action and how quick it was to build a functioning mobile app using our software.

Product demos were our bread and butter. It's what we lived and breathed every working day, so I'm proud to say we got a lot of attention. Mobile marketing was still new, so seeing it in action blew people away. That writer's adage, "show, don't tell," is as true for selling as it is for writing. Let people see what your product does, and the product sells itself. I guess that's why a lot of SaaS businesses now offer free trials.

The guys and I ready to pounce on passersby.

Later that morning, a DEMO rep took me aside to explain how to present. She led me to the auditorium—this huge, cavernous stage surrounded by rows of chairs, and miked me up.

"You're going to come out like this, and then walk over here to the computer," she said, clacking across the stage in high heels. "The computer has a big projector where you can demo your software while talking to the audience. There are a lot of investors here, so keep your pitch tight, and remember your timing. Good luck!"

I looked out at the sea of empty chairs and said, "Yeah, cool, whatever."

Inside, however, I was bubbling with nervous energy. This wasn't a university competition. This was an internationally renowned tech conference. I was presenting to journalists, investors, venture capitalists, engineers, scientists, inventors, economists, and CEOs. I should've been terrified, but I was just too excited, too humbled. I didn't have any notes. I hadn't rehearsed. I was going to freestyle the biggest presentation of my career so far. You know that tickle in your stomach when you climb the first hill of a roller coaster? That's how I felt, only it was a hundred times stronger.

When it was time for us to present, they announced my name, and I had this weird sense of deja vu, like I was at the Entrepreneurship Contest at Chico State all over again. But when I walked on to that floodlit stage, with a huge projector screen behind me and about 600 expectant faces in front, it felt very different indeed. It was like a rock concert or something.

I waited for the audience's polite round of applause to end, and then I said, "Hey, we're here to help make mobile app development easier for small businesses." And at the end of a pretty good demonstration, I said, "Oh, and as we're still

in college, if you want to have a beer, find us in the back."
The whole crowd laughed, and some did join us for a beer.

One of these was a man called Rip Empson.

"Hey, Andrew! What's going on, man?" he said. "Really
liked your presentation."

"Hey, thanks," I said. "Where's your badge?"

"Oh, I don't know. Must've fallen off with all that clapping," he said. "Name's Rip Empson."

"Great to meet you. You want to grab some beers?"

"Sure."

Rip and I got on really well. He was fascinating and had a great sense of humor. After a couple of drinks, he handed me his card and we said goodbye. I didn't even look at it at the time. The one thing you're guaranteed at a conference is a hundred or so business cards. But when we returned to the hotel, I went through them all to remind myself of the people I'd met and came across Rip's. I stared at the card in disbelief, thinking we'd hit the jackpot. Rip was a writer from *TechCrunch*.

Back then, everyone wanted to be in *TechCrunch*. If you were published there, it meant you were going places, and the world took notice. It was one of the biggest brand-building publications around, one of the few PR channels that helped grow your business. In other words, it was the ideal place to launch a startup.

And sure enough, later that evening, Rip wrote, "Hi, Andrew. Great meeting you tonight. I had a ton of fun getting to know you and learning what you're building. You mentioned you're going to be launching your Android app soon, and I'd be interested in writing about it."

We met a lot of people at DEMO and sold a lot of them on the Bizness Apps vision, but meeting Rip did more for us in the early days than any investment could. He wrote about Bizness Apps six or seven times because he loved our story.

We were in college, and we were attacking a big market. We weren't raising money from investors. We were helping small businesses grow and fostering competition.

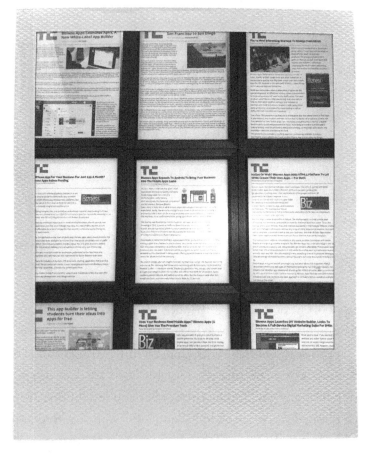

Rip came through for us and helped us spread our story far and wide.

From that point on, everything seemed to go our way. I spent most days blissed out and exhausted, working hard, partying on the weekends, drunk on success. Every day new customers would sign up, and we'd get this metaphorical pat on the back, thinking we were on our way to building a $100 million company. I remember my phone would ping when we were out at bars, and I'd look down to see another customer had signed up. Then the drinks were on us, and our friends would gather around as we clinked glasses and indulged in our success. At twenty years old, wouldn't you have done the same?

When you're young, the world appears to be simple. You think the good times will last forever. Bizness Apps was doing brilliantly for a bootstrapped business in its early years. But we didn't have much competition. We grew quickly because we solved an important problem before anyone else did, but we couldn't maintain the same rate without rethinking our customer acquisition strategy. It's great to call people, meet them, demonstrate your product, and then sign them up, but you can't do that indefinitely. At least, not without hiring a global sales team, which I didn't have the money to do. If I wanted Bizness Apps to scale, if I *really* wanted it to become a $100 million company, or even a million-dollar company, I had to devise a new tactic.

CHAPTER 3

HOW WE SOLVED THE SCALABILITY PROBLEM

AFTER DEMO PUT BIZNESS APPS ON THE MAP, I hired more friends to help capitalize on its momentum. I imagined that a bigger team of cold callers combined with referrals and organic press would multiply our numbers. I couldn't have been more wrong. It wasn't just the pitiful results—my friends couldn't hack it. The swearing, the hang-ups, and the staccato of noes got to them. Close friends—people I'd known for years—walked out on me.

I couldn't blame them. It was a thankless job. Worse, it was mind-numbingly slow. You'd make maybe a hundred calls a day and book just a handful of demos, many of whom would subsequently cancel. That's not to say we weren't doing well before DEMO, but with Zach, Stephen, and I making calls alone, our growth was bottlenecked.

Until then, I'd been focusing on restaurants since that

was the industry where I'd first noticed demand. But trying to get a restaurant manager or owner on the phone was like chasing a chicken around a field. These people were stressed and time-pushed and almost never returned our calls. Even when there was interest, they usually couldn't meet for a week or two. They'd also cancel at any time, which meant hard-won leads often went cold. Eventually, we shifted our focus to other industries. I'd had some success with attorneys and generally the kind of people who were behind desks all day. This doubled our success rate, but in the end, we butted up against the same issue: cold calling was just too damn *slow*.

With competitors sprouting around us like weeds, we had to scale fast, or we'd be jockeying for market share. I didn't want to engage in a marketing or PR war. They're expensive and end up in a race to the bottom. We deserved our space at the top. We had a superior product, were the first to really help businesses, and put our customers' needs first. But like all positions of authority, if they stay empty for too long, you'll find an army of people willing to fill that power vacuum. The clock, therefore, was ticking.

THE CATAPULT

Scaling is all about distribution. You need to find the right channels, the right means, and the right cost. Most successful B2B companies sell in-person, and cold calling opened those doors. But if we wanted to be the number-one mobile app builder in the world, we'd need to sell our apps online or hire a global sales team to continue what my friends and I had been doing in Chico. Being bootstrapped, we didn't have the cash for a "boots on the ground" sales strategy—I'd have blown that $50,000 within weeks. And online selling would be as much of a slog as cold calling. We'd have to hunt customers in over a hundred different countries and then rely on email or international phone calls (potentially in other languages) to sell. This complicated and expensive expansion plan would've left us elbowing for a place among the league of copycats on the horizon.

So what *did* we do? We might've plodded along, slowly exhausting our supply of telephone numbers until someone smarter came along with the right growth strategy and sent us packing. And for a while, we *were* stuck on how to move forward. But I don't believe in leaving anything to chance, so I kept listening to customers as I brainstormed new strategies.

It's important to remember that entrepreneurship isn't a "right time, right place" kind of thing. You have to create your own chances. Importantly, chance favors *action*. I was a nobody, and I still am in the grand scheme of things. I was unexceptional in every possible way. I never had a fortune in the bank to seed my ideas, but I knew what I wanted and put in the hard work to get it. While I was lucky that Bizness Apps launched in tandem with the iPhone, if it hadn't worked out, I'm confident I'd have done something else.

To find solutions to our scalability problem, I read every review, press release, and forum on the industry I could get my hands on. See, ideas are free. To be a successful entrepreneur, you need to play the field a bit and see what people are saying. Eventually, I found the idea for Bizness Apps by watching customer behavior on PhoneFreelancer. Then again, about a year later, one of our customers gave me the key to scaling Bizness Apps.

That's right: customers are surprisingly good problem solvers. They're using the product, after all, and they know things that you might not. In our case, one in particular helped Bizness Apps graduate from a small-town startup to the number-one mobile-app builder in the world.

His name was Raoul Corciulo, owner of a web design company in Switzerland called Vendomat AG. He'd used our platform to build a handful of apps for the multinational hotel chain Ramada, and I thought, *What if we could build all the apps for Ramada? What if this guy has relationships with other hotels we could leverage?* I reached out to Raoul and asked if there was any way we could help him build more apps.

We emailed back and forth for a while, often using Google Translate, as English wasn't Raoul's first language. Finally, Raoul suggested something that would change the course of Bizness Apps forever. This is why you should always listen to your customers. You never know when one of them might change your life.

"Hello, Andrew. Could you white-label the template?"

My first thought was, *What's a white label?*

I looked it up on Wikipedia, and the implications of it were almost too good to be true. We'd license our app-building technology to Raoul. He would slap his branding on it and sell apps to his hospitality customers, and we'd get a 20 to 30 percent commission on the sale. Raul had 200 to 300 hospitality customers, so it was like the solution to the scalability problem had been dropped in my lap. Why labor to build relationships with individual businesses when I could sell to the people who *already had* relationships with those businesses? It was the ideal distribution strategy: the right channel (Bizness Apps earned a global presence almost overnight), the right means (Raoul already had relationships with his customers), and the right cost (it cost us very little to white-label our technology).

Raoul was our first reseller and one of our biggest customers. Later, we would grow to over 5,000 resellers in seventy different countries, with our software available in multiple languages. Our white-label resale partners would walk into small businesses around the globe to sell on our behalf, and we'd earn a commission on every subscription. We didn't pay anything upfront. We didn't need to raise any venture capital. Yet across the world, at all times of the day and night, our people sold to local entrepreneurs and business owners. We may not have had the best product, but we *did* have the best distribution model. It got our apps into more hands than any other app builder in the world.

If you want to sell to small businesses, you need to be the friendly face that pops in to talk to the boss in person. Without an army of salespeople in a bunch of different cities, this was impossible. But the reseller model drastically reduced the number of people to whom we needed to sell. Instead of selling one app at a time for $39 a month, we sold reseller packages for $300 a month to digital agencies (SEO, marketing, design, websites, and so on) with hundreds of customers. We could keep the team small (just me, Zach, Stephen, and my first sales hire, Sam Schnaible, along with some remote engineers I'd found on Upwork) while having an enormous worldwide sales force.

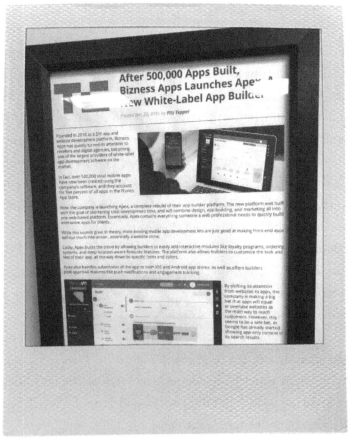

Apex was our all-in-one solution for reseller agencies

Our reseller model put Bizness Apps in front of our target demographic without us ever needing to dial a number or write an email. Resellers loved it too. Every web design agency in the country wanted to add a mobile app to its services. We then partnered with people who would throw webinars and recruit other resellers. We enabled thousands of marketers, agencies, and entrepreneurs to help small businesses build awesome mobile applications, and we couldn't have been happier.

On the back of the reseller program alone, we went from essentially $0 to $5.6 million in annual recurring revenue (ARR) in three years. Typically, it's the other way around: you raise $5 million, and you have $50,000 in revenue. But we had an enormous market and a huge opportunity, and it was the right time, right place. We knew the copiers were coming, so it was a race to scale. If we rose to the top fast enough, we'd earn the brand equity to stay there. Until then, our resellers were mostly inbound leads from *TechCrunch* and Google Ads, but then we hired an outbound sales team to accelerate growth further. This was a team of slick, charming sales folk who'd call every digital agency they could find to say, "Hey, have you ever heard of Bizness Apps? Have you thought about offering mobile apps to your agency services?" By 2014, we'd grown 5,000 percent in just four years, earning our first *Inc.* magazine award as the fifty-eighth fastest-growing company in the US.

When I say entrepreneurship is about making your own luck, I mean it. The moment you commit to a business idea, commit to making it a reality no matter the challenges. Yes, there will be moments when you have to throw in the towel. But don't think of these as failures. Think of them as opportunities to start again stronger than before. The bottom line is this: the harder you work, and the longer you pursue your best ideas, the better your chances are of turning at least one of them into a multimillion-dollar phenomenon.

MORAL OF THE STORY: ASK QUESTIONS

I'd like to close out this chapter with something Christian said after I'd banked his check: "If you ask for advice, you get investment. If you ask for investment, you get advice."

When I met Christian at Tres Hombres, I wasn't thinking about investment. I simply wanted to learn. I remember asking, "How would you grow this business? How would you handle product development? When should I expand to Android?" I wasn't some capricious kid who wanted to make a quick buck but a young, hungry entrepreneur eager to build an amazing business. Christian recognized this, and this was at least partly responsible for him opening his checkbook.

Questions are as responsible for every successful business as the dollars that seed them. Entrepreneurship is about contributing value to the world, and the best way to do that is to question the status quo, ask *why* something is the way it is, or imagine how it might work better. With PhoneFreelancer, I wondered what would happen if I created a template to serve the hundreds of identical app requests I saw every day. The result was Bizness Apps. And then with Bizness Apps, I asked Raoul how I could help him sell more apps. The result was our reseller distribution model.

Inquiry opens doors you might never have known existed. And the best place to start is always with people: your customers, teams, friends, family, colleagues, and professional and social networks. What do they love? What do they complain about? Why do they do the things they do, and *how* do they do them? This might sound a bit trite, but I challenge you to do this and not find a hundred new business ideas.

At the beginning of this chapter, I said every successful startup does three things:

1. Solves a problem or fulfills a need or want

2. Develops a viable business model

3. Tells a great story

I had solved a problem with Bizness Apps. I gave small businesses a chance to compete against their competitors through app-based marketing. Something that would've cost them $100,000 or more in mobile app development cost under $50 per month with us.

I also had a viable business model—a do-it-yourself reseller distribution strategy that cost us nothing but that sold our tech across the world without VC funding or a million-dollar marketing budget.

Now we needed a story. Something that would set us apart

from the copycats. We needed to capture hearts as well as minds. We needed something bigger than ourselves and our technology. We needed a killer hook, a story that customers, press, and the industry as a whole would get behind.

Things were about to heat up at Bizness Apps. When you're bigger, you attract more attention, and that isn't always a good thing. I was used to hard work, but I'd never expected the army of problems that was marching my way: disgruntled staff, feature development, sales strategy, marketing strategy, company operations, server infrastructure, customer support, culture creation, leadership, countless brazen copycats, and the business-killing decision made by Apple and its 4.2.6 rejection.

Also, I'd outgrown Chico. I wanted to go where world-class talent rubbed shoulders with the leading tech companies in the world. And there was only one place to go: the city by the Bay. Little did I know, things were about to get wild.

CHAPTER 4

THE SAN FRANCISCO YEARS

How I Learned What It Means to Be a Good Leader

WITH THE SCALABILITY PROBLEM SOLVED, I was free to focus on other aspects of the business. I'd more or less been running Bizness Apps single-handedly since launch, and I was feeling a bit overwhelmed. There was just so much to do: answering support tickets, making sales calls, and fixing software issues with developers. I was working 100-hour weeks, a slave to my mobile phone, responding to emails as late as one or two in the morning. I can't imagine working that late now, and I certainly wouldn't recommend it, but sometimes you have to do it in order to get the edge you need over your competitors. However, it was difficult to switch off, to give friends and family my undivided attention. I was lucky they understood how much the business meant to me. Many people grow up wanting to be a soccer player or astronaut, but all I wanted was to become CEO, so it never felt like work to me.

Nevertheless, I couldn't have managed those early years without Christian's help. Most investors might check in every quarter, or monthly at most, but I talked to Christian several times a day. At one point, I emailed him more often than his wife or the COO at his billion-dollar business, Build.com, did. You'd think this might've bothered him, but we were great friends, always joking together and having a laugh. It didn't feel like an investor-investee relationship.

But eventually, the calls and emails got a little heavy, and I realized it was time for me to behave more like a CEO and less like someone *playing* CEO. Christian had been a crutch for too long, and I had to step up to bear the weight of Bizness Apps on my own.

But what did a CEO do? I had no idea. I'd never managed teams before, let alone run a company as big as Bizness Apps. Luckily, I had a great mentor in Tim Porthouse, my CEO coach. Tim taught me that CEOs have to fire themselves from everything—from sales to marketing to product development—and then delegate those tasks to other people. I'd been performing all those roles up until then, but as CEO, I had to step back and think about the business holistically: strategy, leadership, culture, and so on. Before I could adopt the role of CEO full time, I had to find people to fulfill the roles I'd been doing on my own—specialists who could build upon the foundations I'd laid so far.

THE RIGHT PEOPLE MAKE A BUSINESS
(THE CHALLENGE IS FINDING THEM)

I had hoped to find my people in Chico. As a college town, it was the ideal launchpad for a startup. It had a ton of young people and a bustling commercial scene thriving on student dollars. As one of the top fifty colleges in the Western region, Chico State attracted students from all over the country, not just California. Each cohort refreshed the local economy and sustained local businesses, many of which had become customers of ours.

What's more, Chico had validated us. It had supplied our first customers and proven our revenue model viable. In our first twelve months, we made $1 million in annual recurring revenue. In the second year, we hit $3 million. Our timing was impeccable. Bizness Apps arrived just as small businesses were figuring out how to leverage a new marketing medium, and with crowds of students arriving every year, Chico was the perfect testing ground.

You'd be forgiven for thinking, then, that Chico would be full of bright-eyed, intelligent graduates desperate to work for an up-and-coming startup. Unfortunately (and this is an issue we'd encounter later too), the best and brightest left for cooler locales and bigger names. I ended up with a team of six, mostly buddies, doing sales calls. Everyone else I had to outsource. I had developers in China, Russia, and Brazil. We were growing so fast I could barely keep up. It was exhausting. I was trying to acquire and delight customers, define our brand and story, research different markets, understand the source of our growth, codify our long-term business strategy, and a million other things while also resolving technical issues with engineers who were in different time zones. What was I missing? Startups thrive when people can bounce ideas off each other, when everyone coalesces around a common goal under expert leadership. We were in a high-growth phase and needed to be as agile as possible, pivoting from one direction to another without skipping a beat.

Yet at the time, most of my team worked remotely, including an engineering team I hadn't properly vetted, given my lack of technical expertise. As a result, I had a ton of coordination issues. Don't get me wrong. I love working with virtual teams. I've always respected freelancers and appreciated their help getting my businesses off the ground. And my clueless hiring strategy did produce the occasional diamond, such as Raymond Chester, who our CTO later said was one of the best developers he'd ever worked with (this was huge praise, given our CTO had worked at several high-profile Silicon Valley businesses).

Back then, however, I'd just give candidates a small project and see how they handled it. I didn't do any code reviews or ask them any technical questions, which meant I'd hire maybe one good coder out of five, and they'd cobble together features and UI with no oversight from anyone who understood what they were doing. In the early days, the quality of the Bizness Apps product wasn't great. It worked. It did some cool things, but it was a far cry from where it should have been. I primarily blame the haphazard approach I took to hiring, a result of my immaturity at the time.

If I wanted to build a world-class team, I needed to look beyond Chico's borders. The obvious choice: San Francisco and the Bay Area. Where else cultivates tech startups better than Silicon Valley, the world-famous stomping grounds of Apple, Facebook, and Google? For years, I'd dreamed of joining this elite club of entrepreneurs whose ideas had led to global domination. You're a small fish when you arrive, and within a year or two you grow into a shark stalking its own territory (or you get eaten by one!). Naturally, I wanted to make a splash with the Valley's strongest swimmers.

But who was I kidding? We didn't have enough money to move Bizness Apps to Silicon Valley. The rents there were ridiculous, even back in 2012. Instead, we moved to Millbrae, a city about a thirty-minute drive northwest of Sunnyvale. It wasn't the epicenter of excellence, but it was a nice spot. Most importantly, we could capitalize on all the talent flocking to the Bay Area for a chance at working on the next unicorn. The Bay Area is like Hollywood in the golden age of cinema, a place where everyone goes to try to make it big. I'd say we're in the golden age of entrepreneurialism, but more on that later.

Our Millbrae office was a huge upgrade from the tiny room we had in Chico, but it was as plain as you could get. I doubt it had been refurbished since the sixties. There were ashtrays in the hallways and "Office Space Available" permanently painted on the outside of the building. But it was cheap, and it was the only office in the area that did month-to-month rent. It probably won't surprise you that "Simple Gaz" was just as frugal in business as his personal life, and the last thing I wanted was to stack fixed costs so early on. We didn't have a receptionist. We didn't have a games room. "We invest money where it matters, and that's in the business," I used to tell the team, which they understood as common sense. We were a startup, and to survive we had to keep costs low.

I ran the business with about $2 million in the company account, which was pure profit from customers. With that kind of money, you might be tempted to pimp out your office as a point of pride or to wow new clients, but in reality, it's a distraction. Customers are your most sustainable source of funding, so that's what we focused on: how could we acquire, delight, and retain customers? How could we help them be more successful? How could we give them the best experience? This was our secret sauce—a mission we kept close to our hearts throughout the early days all the way to acquisition.

BRINGING MY PEOPLE TOGETHER

We arrived in Millbrae with a team of ten. In twelve months, we had a team of thirty. Soon, we occupied three offices in the building, with sales downstairs and everyone else upstairs, including a little snack room. My office was a closet at the end of the hall. Six months later, we'd outgrown Millbrae and moved to 1645 California Street in San Francisco.

Again, our San Francisco office wasn't the nicest in the area. But it was brand new and much larger, which gave the teams room to breathe and left plenty of scope for hiring new people. I still needed to fill my sales, operations, marketing, and engineering teams. And as the company grew, so did the mountain of responsibility towering over me. The business was at a crucial juncture. We were gearing up for explosive growth, and any missteps in my hiring strategy would have long-reaching consequences for our success.

To hire the best candidate, you must first understand the specifics of each job inside and out. If you've done these roles yourself, like I had, defining them is easy. If you haven't, research the role, or better yet, do it for a while. At the very least, talk to and spend time with people who excel in that role, and then you'll know how to spot such talent in the wild.

That said, it wasn't a case of going out and hiring a bunch of C-suite talent with six-figure salaries. Like pimping out an office, hiring the best of the best is an easy way to burn cash.

Instead, I generally looked for three qualities. The first was whether or not the candidate would enjoy working at Bizness Apps. This was the most important, and I'll explain why in a moment. The second was whether or not I'd enjoy working with them. It was rare for anyone to score low on this one, unless they appeared uninterested, unengaged, or overwhelmingly negative. Finally, could they *do* the job? Unless the candidate scored poorly on the previous points, this was probably the easiest to pass. I believed a smart, open, and positive person compensated for lack of experience or skills. Neither my VP of Product nor COO had any prior experience, but they were eager to learn, and over time they became world-class leaders in these roles. This approach hasn't failed me yet.

To my first point, I wanted to hire people who would *enjoy* working at Bizness Apps. This was all about creating the right company culture. I always believed in giving people a chance to do the roles they wanted, regardless of their skillsets. I hired people who were like me: positive, persistent, and believers in what we were doing. I was no expert recruiter, but I knew that if I wanted people to rally around our cause, they had to be like me. While that might sound narcissistic, it meant a lot of people got jobs who otherwise might not have. We never judged candidates by their resumes.

So many companies get this bit wrong, thinking you can stick a bunch of talented people in a room and let nature do the rest. Putting attitude first is crucial because you need these people to help and support each other. Likewise, as CEO, you need to empathize with the people working with you and create the conditions for them to thrive. For most people, it's just a job, and you need to be okay with that. I see a lot of companies insisting the business subsume everything else: personalities, fun, and work-life balance, and their employees rebel because they hate their jobs. I worked long hours because I wanted to, but I didn't expect everyone else to do the same. Everyone has different passions, and they don't always overlap with the work you do.

Nothing like signing up that first customer of the day!

Second, to create the right company culture, it must mirror your values. I focused on creating a culture *I* would want to work in, which meant reflecting my likes and dislikes, as well as what had worked for other companies in the past. My big theme was *positivity*. When things go wrong, I've always tried to gain a broader perspective. I zoom out on my life and focus on how things could be so much worse. If you've got your health, a roof over your head, and food in your belly, you're already doing better than millions of people today and billions of people in the past. Just a hundred years ago, we were facing two world wars, famines, diseases for which we had no cure or vaccination, and countless national crises. But we made it through. I know some people will always think of things in relative terms, and if that's you, just switch your frame of reference. You might not have the most money, the nicest house, the best job (or any job), but things could always be worse. I suppose what really underscores positivity, then, is being thankful for what you have, what's going right for you now, and not letting the bad stuff weigh you down.

When negativity becomes habit, it affects not just you and your mental health but the people around you too. I'm sure you've been in countless meetings where the office drag picked apart your ideas or complained for the umpteenth time about issues over which the company had no control. We all have our off days, but persistent negativity has a devastating effect on productivity. It saps the energy from the room and, worse, blinds people to solutions for the very problems they complain about. Positivity, however, is infectious, and when you're surrounded by optimists, they lift you when things go wrong. If you have a bad sales call, lose a client, or are just feeling a bit blue that day, positive people help you see beyond the fog of disappointment to the happier times ahead.

Positivity makes or breaks great teams.

When ignored, negativity spreads and can reduce productivity by as much as 30 percent.[1] But what happens when people are happy at work, not always because it's their dream career but because they do meaningful work with the support

1   Andra Picincu, "The Effects of Negativity in the Workplace," *Chron*, July 27, 2020, https://smallbusiness.chron.com/effects-negativity-workplace-11655.html.

of their teams? Companies with engaged employees outperform those without by 202 percent,[2] *and* they put double the effort in too. In other words, positivity creates happy, loyal, and motivated teams.

One of my favorite quotes from Michael Jordan is, "Talent wins games, but teamwork wins championships." Company culture is all about the long game, and when you get it right, people stick around. Most companies in the Bay Area retained people for maybe one or two years. Our people stayed for five to six. Some started with me in Chico and stayed until Bizness Apps was acquired—a span of over ten years.

With a bedrock of positivity, it's easier for everyone to focus on the same goal. Lots of books tell you to codify your company's mission and values to keep you focused on the right things. When you do this, it helps attract and retain people, too, as well as providing context and direction for new starters. Our mission was to help small businesses succeed, and it informed everything we did. You'd be surprised how often we encountered deadlocks, and it was only in referring to our mission that we were able to pick the best path going forward. It's your North Star. No matter how the world changes around you, the mission keeps you on track.

---

2   Bulent Osman, "Reversing Low Employee Engagement in Manufacturing," *Forbes*, April 17, 2018, https://www.forbes.com/sites/forbestechcouncil/2018/04/17/reversing-low-employee-engagement-in-manufacturing.

Halloween was always a big deal at Bizness Apps.

The final quality I looked for in a candidate was whether or not they could *do* the job. Again, this was the easiest to pass if I knew I wanted to work with them and they wanted to work for Bizness Apps. If you had the right attitude and motivation, our training programs would do the rest. We recruited for entry-level positions and then trained people up and let them carve out roles and increase their levels of responsibility as they learned what to do. I can't overstate how much this impacted job satisfaction.

Overall, it's important to give people space to grow. I spent a lot of time with my team, getting to know them personally and professionally. I never thought of them as employees but as friends, which might go against every leadership book ever written. But I didn't care (still don't!). I made lifelong friends at Bizness Apps. I speak to my former CFO all the time. They were family to me. They could've worked anywhere, and instead they chose to work with me, so I treated them with the respect and love they deserved, and I got the same in return.

I don't think there was anything magical or fortuitous about this. If you pick the right people, nurture them, and give them the conditions to flourish, they'll surprise you (and themselves). This is its own reward. There's nothing like watching someone chisel out space for themselves. It's tempting to think it's your job to define that space, but the more room you give them, the fewer limits you place on their role or career path, the better they perform (which boosts your bottom line).

BEING AN EFFECTIVE CEO

Some people think being CEO means standing at the stern cracking a whip. But to me, you're there to hire a great team, create a great work environment, and then fend off everything that impedes your team's progress. You're the navigator: you set the direction, and the team propels you forward. You ensure safe passage either by removing obstacles to your team's goals or charting a course around them. To do this, you need to communicate with your teams, and in the right way.

Not your usual company conference.

I had regular meetings where the goal was to help my teams do their jobs better. It was never, "Hey, why haven't you done this? I told you to do this, so what's the problem?" That's not leadership; it's dictatorship. Instead, I wanted to encourage and inspire my teams, to fight alongside them. "How can I help you do the best job? What resources are you lacking? What are you considering as a strategy? Would you like my opinion on anything?" It's questions like these that help people do their jobs.

If you micromanage people, they lose autonomy, and with it, motivation. Why forge ahead when you've got someone second-guessing your every move? If you make everyone's decisions for them, people lose their capacity for independent thought. It belittles their jobs and devalues their input, and they dread coming to work because it's a tedious slog rather than a stimulating challenge. If you think being CEO is about power, you'll lose it. Let people do their jobs. Trust your hiring strategy. Trust your talent. Relinquish control of important tasks to people who can focus on them full time; otherwise, you'll leak talent, money, *and* customers.

One of my costliest mistakes was starting a $100,000-per-month pay-per-click Google Ads campaign without having someone analyze its performance. In the early days, we didn't know the source of our signups. We didn't have any analytics telling us this lead came from Google, this came from a referral, and so on. I didn't have time to figure it all out either. The customers were rolling in, so I thought it better to leave things alone unless we discovered a problem. Bad idea. I call it the era of "blowing up a Ferrari every month." When we hired someone to analyze the source of our leads, they concluded the Google campaign was a waste of money. Had I maintained control over our marketing strategy, who knows how much money I'd have blown.

Marketing hadn't been our only problem either. Back in 2011, Amazon Web Services wasn't as widely used as it is today. If you needed servers, you rented them from companies that had the hardware. Cloud hosting was still fairly new, so we relied on servers rented from firms in Texas and Chicago. This was the best we could afford, and it was adequate for our needs at the time. As we grew, however, it quickly became clear our hosting arrangement was unscalable. Once millions of people were downloading and using our apps, choke points emerged, and our servers broke down.

When the servers went down, everything crashed. Our clients couldn't build apps. We couldn't add new features or release bug fixes. Worst of all, our clients' customers couldn't use their mobile apps. It was a nightmare. Whenever it happened, I'd be on the phone all day persuading customers to stick with us. Our remote engineers spent most of their time deploying fixes instead of developing the software, none of which solved the underlying problem. Over time, our architecture grew convoluted and messy—a wheezing, creaking, duct-taped engine that threatened to blow up at any moment (and did several times!). Eventually, I hired a VP of Engineering and a team of in-house developers and got them to rewrite the architecture to handle millions of people accessing it at once. It was a tough transition, but we got there.

Being CEO wasn't just about fixing problems, however. It was also about setting an example when things got tough. Bizness Apps wasn't the first mobile app builder, and it certainly hasn't been the last. We were among the first to do it well, and this gave us relatively easy pickings in the early days. Yet as we grew, our success put a target on our backs. Entrepreneurs were watching our every move and soon began copying our business model. Their tactics were pretty underhanded. I remember at least three companies that signed up as resellers, deconstructed our software, and then copied it verbatim. I used to find lines of our code inside their software. And the crazy part? They were really successful—some became million-dollar businesses.

Another CEO might've blown their top and litigated the hell out of these pretenders. There's an ocean of difference between improving on an established business model and straight-up copying it. But taking legal action can distract from running your business. They also get the satisfaction of knowing that it bothers you and might even steal your market share while you're blustering over lawsuits and copyright. Running a business is a psychological game as much as an intellectual one. You want to galvanize your teams for struggles like these and thicken their skin until it's as tough as bark. "If they're spending money educating the market on mobile applications, we benefit because we have the best product in the market, hands down," I told my teams. And it was true:

we were five years ahead of everybody, generating ten times the revenue. Our positive culture and tightly focused mission insulated us from distractions and kept us sharp, cool, and composed. And that's the only way to win.

The thing is, there are very few truly unique ideas anymore. Your best bet is to find somewhere to add value and then double down on the things your competitors miss or do poorly. Make something easier, cheaper, faster, or more accessible. That's what I did for mobile apps for small businesses. It's pretty reprehensible to steal someone else's work, but if you can see a way of doing it better, go out and do it. That's how business and competition work, after all.

If no one copies you, you're not trying hard enough. You have to own it. You tell customers, "No, we're not the cheapest, but we're the leader in the market. We've been the leader in the market for the past seven years. I'm sure you're looking at other companies, but here's how we do things differently." Customers chose us because we had the best customer support, the best product, and the best reseller program. So whenever I heard of a new company riding on our coattails, I was more flattered than flustered. I remember appearing on bestselling author Nathan Latka's podcast, talking about one of our first copycats, BuildFire. He'd written a chapter in his book "How to Be A Capitalist Without Any Capital" about how to get rich copying other companies' ideas and had used Bizness Apps and BuildFire as an example. Nathan was keen to know how I handled it and probably wondered what I thought of his book. I said, "If someone thinks my idea is worth copying, they're more than welcome to try." Not the sassiest of replies, but I meant it. Competition is good for everyone. We stayed in the new San Francisco office for about four years. They were great times. You could call it the honeymoon period. We were signing up hundreds of new customers a day, hiring lots of people, and generally enjoying the ride. As CEO, I'd done well thanks to mentors like Christian Friedland and Tim Porthouse. We'd created the right culture and were developing a story people cared about.

Now let me explain how that story developed—how we finally won over the hearts and minds of not just customers but the press too.

CHAPTER 5

THE SAN FRANCISCO YEARS

How I Learned the Value of Storytelling

WHEN WE THINK OF STORIES, WE THINK OF PEOPLE. For me, it was my family. My dad passed away when I was six, and my mom worked her fingers to the bone to support us. She didn't have a college education, and she needed a flexible job where she could raise my brother and me while still putting food on the table, so she cleaned houses. We struggled for a long while. We were even on food stamps. The irony was we lived in San Clemente, which is a beautiful beach town shimmering with material wealth. I remember thinking, *Why can't we go on vacation to Hawaii for spring break like everyone else? Oh, that's right, we don't have any money.* It was then that I realized that money was freedom, that I needed to build wealth so my family wouldn't struggle anymore and my own children wouldn't grow up worrying whether the paycheck would stretch to new school shoes.

My mom eventually got remarried to a painter and decorator who ran a small business with a handful of employees. He worked long hours for little pay, so we were still living month to month. To this day, my mom and stepdad have never been able to save anything. I always thought it was weird when other kids' parents had "proper" jobs at big companies where they wore dress suits to fancy offices and drove company cars. My parents, on the other hand, would bus home, spattered in bleach or paint, having toiled ten to fourteen hours to scrape together enough money for the family to live on. They weren't fortunate enough to have had a college education or to be hoisted on the first rung of the corporate career ladder.

Even so, it would be remiss of me to suggest it was all bad. My parents weren't shackled to a desk or verbally whipped by some ambitious middle manager. They were independent and respected by clients for giving outstanding service. My stepdad was a craftsman who took great care and delight in his work. Even my mom was proud to be her own boss. The truth is, small businesses are the bedrock of America. My parents' jobs might've sounded tough, but there are plenty of people who'd love to do what they did.

And this is where the seed of the Bizness Apps story germinates. It's a story of David vs. Goliath, of small businesses standing up for their place in the American economy against corporate behemoths that would just as soon as swallow them whole.

There are many variations of this in the business world, and we certainly weren't the first to use it. Nevertheless, as a bootstrapped business, storytelling was an early customer acquisition strategy that became our most powerful sales tool. At our peak, Bizness Apps had around 50 million monthly active customers. But that's nothing. The market research firm Statista reports there were 3.5 *billion* smartphone users in 2020. Just think about that for a moment. Almost half the world's population owns a smartphone, a portable gateway to the entirety of the internet.

You see, stories are more than just bedtime entertainment. They're our way of making sense of a complex, dynamic world. Without stories, we'd drown in our own data. Every day, the world creates around 2.5 exabytes of new information (2.5 million terabytes).[3] Can't visualize that? Try this: it's over double the data siloed in the world's biggest web servers (Amazon, Google, Facebook, and Microsoft).

Think of all the mediums we're exposed to: ads (digital and physical), radio, TV, websites, podcasts, books, ebooks, movies, blogs, newspapers, magazines, and a hundred other formats. Even if your brain ran on full capacity, processing 120 bits per second[4] over sixteen hours (assuming eight hours of sleep), you would consciously process just under a megabyte of data per day, or about as much as a four-megapixel JPEG.

---

3   "Data Never Sleeps 5.0," Domo, accessed July 31, 2021, https://www.domo.com/learn/data-never-sleeps-5.

4   Daniel J. Levitin, "Why It's So Hard To Pay Attention, Explained By Science," *Fast Company*, September 23, 2015, https://www.fastcompany.com/3051417/why-its-so-hard-to-pay-attention-explained-by-science.

We've always had this limitation. Long before computers, the internet, or writing were invented, we used stories—meaningful connections of ideas—to pass traditions, histories, and knowledge from one generation to the next.

Today, some people think of stories as entertainment and escapism, but the right story can also help businesses transcend the noise of today's information age. Think of mnemonics and other learning devices—our brain's desire for order out of the chaos makes these techniques useful. Rather than pitching a list of benefits to your customers, you must introduce them as protagonists in a much larger story.

Take that earlier example. You probably can't imagine the vastness of 2.5 exabytes of data. But comparing that number to the largest web servers in the world, your mind pictures endless warehouses of towering, blinking server stacks. In other words, you created a story to contextualize that 2.5-exabyte number, a story involving a global network of physical spaces, which is much easier to grasp than its virtual equivalent.

The same applies to business messages. Consider the following:

1,000 songs in your pocket.

An MP3 player with 5GB storage.

Which is the more memorable? Which makes the benefit come alive?

Apple's famous iPod slogan above is the perfect example of the power of storytelling. It says, "Take your record collection with you wherever you go, and soundtrack your life with an endless stream of your favorite music." It contextualizes its key features so anyone, regardless of technical background, can grasp them. The alternative simply describes a device, a thing, and you have to work harder to understand what it means: *What's an MP3? Is 5GB storage enough?* and so on.

If you want a strong, memorable brand, you need a strong, memorable story, and that's what we developed with Bizness Apps. Your brand and story are interconnected, often referred to as your *brand story*. Unlike a story you might read in a book, brand stories don't end. There are no winners or losers, just the story gathering pace and evolving. If your story ends, so does your raison d'etre, so expect your story to change as the market and world change around you.

THE EVOLUTION OF OUR STORY

Our first attempt at a story was explaining what an iPhone app was. What does this thing do? Why should you have one? So we focused on defining the problems we could solve. One of those was helping businesses connect with their customers through their mobile devices. Everyone was on their mobile phones, spending hours each day using apps, taking photos and videos, and messaging friends and family. "Connect with your customers where they are: on their mobile phones," we told our clients. To them it made sense: the smartphone was the most in-demand technology of the time.

Then we developed the story further. You never get your strategic narrative correct the first time. You just try one and see how people respond. Our story evolved from the benefits of creating an app to the benefits of creating one using our technology. We talked about simplifying mobile app development and making it affordable and easy for small businesses, no matter the size or budget. We asked people to pick a side: do it the hard, expensive way (which no one wants to do), or do it the easy, affordable way. You could build an iPhone app with us for under $50 per month (the price of a newspaper ad) without any help or coding experience in a single day. The alternative? Hire a developer who'd spend months building your app and charge you up to $100,000. We made a complex, expensive process faster, cheaper, and easier, which was an irresistible story in the world of technology. Publications like *TechCrunch* ate it up.

As our tech story gained traction, we began thinking of a story with broader appeal. We wanted to attract the likes of *Inc.*, *Entrepreneur*, and *Forbes*, and a simple "we do it better" message wouldn't cut it. We stopped thinking so much about *what* we did but rather *why* we did it. It didn't take much introspection to realize I'd had the right story imprinted in me from my childhood: we were helping small businesses compete with big businesses. I wanted to give people like my parents more solid footing through mobile marketing. Again, we wanted people to pick sides: was it fair that Starbucks could build a multimillion-dollar mobile app so you could order a latte through your phone, but your local coffee shop couldn't? Why didn't every small business have the means to build a powerful way to connect with their customers?

Bizness Apps wasn't the first app builder, but it did make it super easy to build one. Before us, you could build anything from a restaurant app to a mobile game, but you had to be a developer. We gave small businesses the tools to customize and build any app they wanted without having to write a single line of code. They didn't need to spend tens of thousands of dollars on app development. They could do it with us for less than fifty bucks a month. We gave local businesses a fighting chance against the global megabrands stealing their market share. This was our David-and-Goliath story.

Small businesses are the backbone of healthy, diverse economies. Monopolies, on the other hand, service the lowest common denominator, boring consumers with bland, soulless experiences. With Bizness Apps, small businesses could create a customized app as good as anything the big players produced, but for a fraction of the time and cost. In other words, we helped support a thriving, competitive economy where every business, no matter how small, could compete in the medium of the moment: mobile phones. I believed in what we were doing. We weren't making another Snapchat; we were making something that democratized entrepreneurship and put every local business in the pockets of its customers. People bought into it emotionally. Not just customers, but my whole team. We were excited and motivated, and the work was meaningful.

The agencies we worked with, our resellers and so on, loved this story too. Many of their clients were small businesses, so when they learned our product could help their clients compete against megabrands in their local communities, the response was incredible. As we grew, we took our partners and agencies and their clients with us—everyone shared in our success. Bizness Apps was a force of change, a juggernaut leveling the mobile marketing playing field. Soon, our story was in *The Wall Street Journal, The New York Times, VentureBeat, Forbes, TechCrunch, Inc.*, and every single news outlet we could find.

According to Harvard researcher Gerald Zaltman, 95 percent of purchase decisions are emotional ones.[5] We really tapped into that. We weren't selling a product; we were helping people. That subtle distinction reshapes how you communicate and alters customers' perception of you. People were proud to work with Bizness Apps because we were helping small businesses, the backbone of the United States economy—the *global* economy—succeed.

HOW WE TOLD IT

Getting your story right is just half the battle. You also need to get it out there. We couldn't afford PR or digital marketing agencies to do the grunt work for us. We pitched every new product launch or milestone to every reporter. We *hounded*

---

5   Logan Chierotti, "Harvard Professor Says 95% of Purchasing Decisions Are Subconscious," *Inc.*, March 26, 2018, https://www.inc.com/logan-chierotti/harvard-professor-says-95-of-purchasing-decisions-are-subconscious.html.

these poor journalists. Anything remotely newsworthy, we pitched. We picked up a lot of organic press (coverage we didn't have to pitch for) too. As our brand grew, we began to appear in articles like, "The Top 10 Mobile App Builders," "The Best Tools to Help You Go Mobile," and so on, which is perhaps unsurprising given every mainstream business publication had received at least one email from us. *Entrepreneur* published our stories in their print and online magazines, which was a proud moment, as I'd been reading the magazine since high school.

Our press outreach wasn't always successful, however. Often, I'd chase a reporter for two months with the same story. "Hey, it's an exclusive," I'd tell them, which almost guaranteed they'd at least listen to my pitch. Building a relationship with a reporter is critical. It's just like sales. You have to sell your story over the hundred other stories that were pitched that morning. They have to like you. I tried to be myself and less like a corporate shill demanding free press. I didn't take myself too seriously. I said dumb things like, "Yo, what up, *TechCrunch?* I have the best pitch you'll hear in your entire life," just to stand out from the crowd. One time a reporter said, "Hey, we're going to pass, but I actually laughed. That was kind of funny. Thanks for sending it, but it's a no for now." If you can stand out just a little bit, you'll get a much better response rate.

Pitch your story often too. Don't rely on one reporter, but foster relationships with many of them. That way, when you have something newsworthy to report, you multiply your chances of publication. But if you haven't articulated your story properly, haven't tested it with customers, or haven't reached out to any reporters, you won't get any press at all.

We won Inc. Magazine's 500 Fastest-Growing Companies twice in a row.

In 2015, I applied for *Inc.*'s 30 Under 30 award. This was less about vanity and more about achieving some high-level exposure. First, you answer some general questions over email. Then one of their reporters interviews you by phone for about twenty minutes. They want to know what you do, what your vision is, how big the company is, and so on. All very casual. They also ask about revenue and expect it to be audited by an ARC accountant or tax firm, just to prove you're the real deal.

We went through the same thing for *Inc.*'s 500 fastest-growing companies. We won that twice in a row but had to stop applying because our financial data was encouraging copycats. The more press we got, the more people would think, *Wow these guys are growing like crazy—let's do what they do!* Perhaps if we'd had a tougher business model to emulate, we might've won more awards.

In 2016, I joined the Forbes Technology Council, a Forbes column written by tech entrepreneurs. *Forbes* has been a global authority on all things business for over a century, so this was a big win for us. It boosted our credibility, amplified our voice, and allowed us to publish on our own schedule.

That said, it was fair to assume that many of our prospects weren't browsing *Forbes* or *Entrepreneur* with their morning coffee. While press coverage gets you a fat stamp of approval from the industry, it doesn't necessarily put you in front of your customers. How could we tell our story to prospects *and* entice them to try us out?

Our answer was that we had to be the number-one search result online for every question related to mobile or mobile marketing. That way we'd not only reach our target audience, but if we also delivered the best answers to their queries, we could convince them to sign up. This turned into a long-term, content-driven growth strategy that ran parallel to press outreach.

We produced a prodigious amount of content: blogs, infographics, videos, tutorials, emails, ebooks, audio, case studies—you name it, we made it. We joined every mobile marketing conversation in the industry. Every year, we'd issue our top ten or twenty mobile marketing trends. We wrote about small business trends, consumer trends, industry news, customer loyalty programs, and other topics relevant to our customers. This is where search engine optimization (SEO) shines: it's not what people type into a search engine that's important but what it reveals about their problems, opinions, and behavior. Forget keyword stuffing and instead create content that serves the intention behind those keywords. Not only does this produce an unlimited supply of new content ideas, but the better you serve that intention, the more helpful your content is, resulting in greater trust and credibility.

We spoke about mobile technology and small business across so many different platforms we were like a media company. If you googled a question related to mobile—how push notifications work or something—we'd be on the first page of results, usually in the top five. We helped businesses even if they weren't interested in our product. You might've heard the term "inbound marketing." HubSpot coined it, I think, but we were obsessive about that strategy. With stories, you have to commit. You need to research what your target audience wants to know, what problems they have, and how they feel about different topics and then produce well-written, relevant, and helpful content around those areas. If you were a small business, for example, you'd read blog articles like "7 Tips to Boost Your Small Business Marketing." If you were a mobile developer, you'd read blog articles like "How To Sell Apps to Real Estate Agents." We became the authority on these topics to drive inbound traffic we could then convert into customers.

I could write about stories all day long, but I've still got the Bizness Apps one to tell. So let me sum up this chapter with a few key points. Stories epitomize your business mission. They elicit an emotional response from customers, employees, stakeholders, the press, and everyone else, which makes them powerful motivators. However, great stories don't spring out of nowhere unless you're extraordinarily lucky. Instead, you have to publish as many variants as you can to see which ones people love.

It's okay to change your narrative over time, but understand who your audience is and what they want. Your story needn't be unique (David vs. Goliath certainly wasn't), but it must have a new angle. Then, when you hit upon that one inspiring narrative, tell it in a hundred different ways. Get in touch with every journalist and publication in your field, and push the story as much as you can. Publish content that helps the key players in your story. Assert yourself as an authority on the topics your customers care about most.

Do all of this and growth will explode. But as you're about to discover, growth isn't everything. In fact, the Bizness Apps rocket ship was beginning to run out of fuel. When you reach a certain size, your customer pools empty, and it becomes harder and more expensive to refill them. I had a choice to make: raise funds or raise profits. Move up or move out. Join me as I explain how leaving San Francisco was the first step toward a life-changing acquisition.

CHAPTER 6

THE SAN DIEGO YEARS

From Growth to Profitability

HAVE YOU EVER ENJOYED SOMETHING SO MUCH YOU continued doing it despite your mind or body telling you to stop? In some ways, this is what drives success—that determination to keep going forward no matter the odds or the impact on your well-being. However, there's a fine line between obsession and determination. After seven years or so of being at the Bizness Apps helm, I was beginning to feel exhausted, both mentally and physically. I put this down to having done too much for too long, to not delegating early enough. I wasn't that same kid who'd started a company in his dorm room; I was a bona fide CEO with the battle scars to prove it. I began to wonder how I could have done things differently, and I extrapolated what I'd learned into several possible futures. The long slog for growth, though ultimately successful, had left me reeling. Did I want to continue this march forward or change tactics?

Things were getting tough. As Bizness Apps scaled, we hit the law of diminishing returns. We'd exhausted our usual sales channels and had to pay more to get the same results. Think about it: when you scoop peanut butter out of a jar, it's easy at first. You can get those big, delicious spoonfuls. Later, you have to work your spoon around the outside, scraping away at the crust. It's the same with sales. Once you've exhausted your supply of ready buyers, you have to work harder—you need to sell to the fence-sitters, the stragglers, and the cost-conscious. These are tougher nuts to crack, so you need to rethink your strategy or find new markets or channels to exploit.

With venture capital, you can build an outbound sales team to call every business in the country (which we also did but not at venture scale). However, we had to use cost-effective strategies that had limitations. Although we dominated the search engines for mobile marketing, there were only so many people interested in that topic. To reach others, you need to start conversations over email, phone, or face-to-face meetings. Growth then becomes a function of the size of your target market and the number of salespeople you have. We couldn't afford an aggressive push campaign. Instead, we focused on bringing people to us through content, partnerships, our reseller network, branding, and so on, which grew less effective over time.

It was strange seeing my own exhaustion reflected in the market. It's a problem that creeps up on you. You might not catch on until *after* you've lost money, and then you have to throw more money at the problem to counter its effects. But when you double down on marketing spend or hire more salespeople, all you're doing is multiplying your expenses. It's the metaphorical equivalent of chasing your tail.

We kept an eye on this through a metric called churn. This determines how many new customers you must find to replace the ones that leave you. Our churn rate was low most of the time, around 2 to 3 percent per month, but that meant replacing 20 to 30 percent of our revenue every year. This is typical of businesses that sell to small to medium enterprises (SMEs). And as you grow, it becomes harder to replace that revenue. You need to inject more money to maintain your growth rate.

Most startups resort to fundraising at this point. Like all young CEOs in the heart of Startupland, I considered it too.

VC FUNDING VS. BOOTSTRAPPING

At first, I met with venture capitalist (VC) firms like Sequoia, Battery, Accel, Emergence, Bessemer—everyone on Sandhill Road in Silicon Valley.

Four years in San Francisco had passed. I had a choice to make: do we grow at the same rate and jeopardize profits, raise VC funding and lose autonomy, or rethink expenses to continue growing sustainably?

It's a question every startup faces at one time or another, and how you respond determines the future of your company.

I've seen growth-focused startups burn fast and bright like a meteor and then vanish forever. I've also seen startups that focus on profitability smolder away without ever achieving the fiery momentum to attract acquisition. Between these two extremes lie profitable startups that grow sustainably and are later acquired for millions of dollars—and that's what I wanted for my company.

Here's a tip: if you want VC funding, the best time to raise money is when you don't need it. That way you have all the leverage. I'd grown Bizness Apps sustainably. We were hugely profitable, which was virtually unheard of in Silicon Valley. One of our best profitability decisions, for example, was charging a yearly subscription. If it cost $600 to acquire a customer and we charged an annual fee of $5,000 upfront, we instantly profited from the acquisition.

We call this the customer acquisition cost (CAC) payback period. With a short CAC payback period, we generated instant profit, which was then reinvested in the business to fuel further growth. We secured several six-figure partnerships with public companies using this model. And for a long time, this worked. We had far more spare cash than other VC-funded businesses in Silicon Valley, and that made us an attractive prospect for venture capitalists.

The first meeting I ever had with a VC was at our shabby office in Millbrae. It was after 7:00 p.m. and I was the only one there. Christian had called Jeremy Levine and asked him to visit, primarily to get a lift to the airport. I had no idea who Jeremy was, but he showed up to my seventies-throwback office with ashtrays in the halls and introduced himself. I suggested we grab a quick dinner at In-N-Out across the street (it's like a better version of McDonald's), and while we were munching burgers and guzzling soda I asked him, completely unprepared for his reply, "What was your favorite investment?"

Jeremy wiped his mouth with his napkin and said, "So there's this five-person company. I loved the founders and made an investment in them. They're called Yelp." Then he talked about his investments in Pinterest and Shopify. I couldn't believe it. Here was a top-ten VC eating at In-N-Out with me and telling stories about meeting founders of billion-dollar companies in their garage. He was a cool guy, and humble. I still exchange emails with him every once in a while, usually along the lines of, "Hey, Jeremy, do you remember me? We ate at In-N-Out one time," because who goes to In-N-Out with a VC of his caliber without knowing who he is?

Later, I got friendly with another well-known VC who'd invested early in several public software companies. He sent me a term sheet (similar to a letter of intent) outlining a multimillion-dollar investment deal for Bizness Apps.

While a term sheet isn't legally binding, it showed how serious he was, and I was humbled to receive an offer from one of Silicon Valley's most well-respected venture capitalists. I called him the next day and said, "Thanks, but I wouldn't know what to do with all that money." He was a bit surprised, as it's not too often young entrepreneurs turn down large investment offers. But he understood and respected my decision, and we've been friends ever since.

Here's the problem. Today, founders gloat more about funding than they do about profits. They believe if you throw enough money into scaling, you can avoid profitability altogether (at least in the short term). Uber, Spotify, Snap, Lyft, WeWork, and so on are just a few examples of companies that chose growth at any cost. However, only 7 percent of startups make it to a valuation or sale of over $40 million, and only 1.28 percent of startups achieve a billion-dollar valuation.[6] Ignoring profitability can, therefore, have devastating consequences, and it calls our whole funding culture into question.

Don't get me wrong: I understand why some startups raise funding. It allows you to hire the best teams and spend a fortune on advertising. You also benefit from the mentorship of people who know more about entrepreneurship than you do. On the flip side, a huge cash injection is like fueling a rocket ship with nitrogen tetroxide. If you don't have everything right from the beginning, you'll veer dangerously off course or explode in a fiery ball of missed opportunity. You need to have product-market fit and happy customers and know how to capitalize on these advantages quickly, or you could be in a lot of trouble. If you hire fifty or a hundred people and growth falters, morale suffers, which in turn worsens results.

Some people want to build a company with a thousand people, take it public, and raise funding, but having met many of them in Silicon Valley, I didn't envy them at all. They were

---

6 "Your Startup Has a 1.28% Chance of Becoming a Unicorn," CB Insights, May 25, 2015, https://www.cbinsights.com/research/unicorn-conversion-rate.

working in such different conditions, under so much pressure. You were introduced to them at a meetup or conference, and they had this frantic, harried look about them. They were chained to the whims of others, no longer in charge of their own destinies. It reminded me of old fears. Back in college, it was that of a boss dictating my every move. In Silicon Valley, it was the fear of a board doing the same. To me, there was no fun in that.

Once you accept investment and the crazy growth goals attached to it, you're sucked into a fundraising loop. It's like building a house on sand. The taller you build, the further you sink, so you get caught in this never-ending cycle of spending, growing, and raising funding. Series A becomes series B. Series B becomes series C. And so on until you spend all your time raising capital instead of helping customers. Your success as an entrepreneur is then defined by how well you can raise money, not your ability to build a healthy, sustainable business.

I always wanted to build a profitable company. When your business is profitable, you're in control of its destiny. We did have some early angel investors, but they were very hands-off. I owned about 90 percent of the company, and voting was based on ownership. Even though I was serious about showing a return on investment, I was free to take the company in any direction I wanted. I didn't want a board of directors telling me what to do, what I could spend, or who I could hire. I didn't want venture capitalists dictating our direction or fundraising to distract from running my business. Nor did I want to exchange equity for cash when I could grow the business without any cash at all. I wanted autonomy, and bootstrapping was the way to do it.

It was so much fun running the company this way. Fun is important. If you hate what you do or are always under stress, what's the point?

Also, bootstrapping has its own advantages. I wrote about them in VentureBeat and Gigaom. I won't go into lots of detail here (you can read the articles in the resources chapters), but to summarize, bootstrapping makes you smarter. You listen more to customers and focus on their needs above everything else. As a result, you end up building a better product and providing a better service. Customers are your most sustainable source of funding, so it makes sense to build your company around them, not investors.

If investor funding cushions every blow, every setback, you become complacent and overfocused on short-term wins. You tend to spend your way out of problems instead of solving them. And with boards hampering your decision-making, you become less agile, less responsive, which means spending more money on growth and more rounds of funding to replace those wasted dollars.

Bootstrapping, on the other hand, breeds a culture of efficiency, creativity, and problem-solving. Without investor dollars, you succeed or fail based on how well your product performs, how quickly you can get it in the hands of your customers, and how fast you can respond to their feedback. Everyone in the business has a role and understands how that role contributes to the success of the business. When something goes wrong, you fix it or try something new. Customers become your sole focus—your only source of funding. We bent over backward to help new customers set up their mobile apps, knowing we wouldn't have a second chance. The extra effort paid off. Not only did this help improve our product and win new customers, but we gained invaluable feedback along the way.

Bizness Apps started with a check for $50,000. We'd made it to Silicon Valley on our own. This made us an extraordinarily tight-knit and focused team. We ran the business efficiently because we had to. We had a very narrow margin for error. We were obsessive about everything. Every customer mattered. Every sales call mattered. Every feature mattered. We were lean and agile and accounted for every cent. People loved that sense of focus. We never spent our way out of problems. And without a VC fund's obscene growth goals, we could stay small and scrappy while still bumping up our numbers.

Companies like Squarespace, WuFoo, Braintree, Lynda.com, 37 Signals, Campaign Monitor, and Github all bootstrapped their way up. If they could do it, why couldn't we?

SUSTAINABLE BOOTSTRAPPING: OUR MOVE TO SAN DIEGO

With VC funding crossed off the list, I had to rethink our expenses. We would focus on being as efficient as possible, and that meant moving away from Silicon Valley to a place where we could continue doing what we did best at a fraction of the budget.

I had an ulterior motive for this too. I'd had a few acquisition offers for Bizness Apps while we were in San Francisco, none of which I considered seriously, but it did get me thinking seriously about acquisition. If I were to sell Bizness Apps in a few years, I'd attract better offers if it was larger and more profitable. Without funding, it would be impossible to achieve either goal in San Francisco, but I could do it somewhere cheaper.

The Bay Area is a crazy place. It attracts more VC funding than any other region in the US, but it's also the second most expensive city to live in. I don't envy founders who go down the VC route. Imagine the dilemma: you want to reduce costs, but you want the funding too. Relocating to raise funding means shipping yourself *and* your employees to one of the most expensive places in the country with no guarantees. You must be able to afford to pay wages commensurate with the cost of living or you just won't attract the right people.

For a bootstrapped company like ours, it was hard to pay the salaries San Francisco demanded. According to the MIT living wage calculator, the average two-bedroom apartment hovers around $4,200 per month, making it difficult to justify living there unless you're raking in hundreds of thousands of dollars per year. As such, the top talent wanted to work for big names like Facebook, Google, Salesforce, Dropbox, Apple, and other well-funded startups. The VC-backed startups and billion-dollar companies recruited the best before they'd even set foot in the job market. In other words, we got whatever the likes of Apple, Facebook, or Google didn't want. While we recruited some awesome people in San Francisco, top-tier

C-suite candidates were a rare find. Bizness Apps was doing well, but the cost of being in San Francisco, bidding against billion-dollar businesses for the best talent, was leaching profitability and stunting our capacity for growth.

Breaking ground in San Francisco is like digging frozen soil. You labor away for months with little progress, no matter how hard you swing your pickax. Our chances were much better elsewhere, where there was less competition for talent. With a global marketplace and high-speed internet, physically being where your customers are is less important. Switching to an up-and-coming city with lower living costs instantly boosts profits since you spend less on rent and salaries and can hire better talent. With more money to play with, you can also provide them a much better working environment and improve their package benefits.

Moving the company was a bold decision, however, and I needed advice. I called Christian one day and said, "Hey, Chris, so I've been thinking about moving the business out of the Bay Area."

There was a brief pause in which I could hear the murmur of office chatter. In that second or so, I wondered whether Christian's inner investor would take leaving San Francisco as a sign things had gone wrong.

"About time," he said, and we both laughed.

Christian, of course, knew of the challenges we faced in San Francisco, but I think he was also thinking of me. Although we rarely spoke of it, Christian could see I was running on empty. San Francisco had chewed me up and spit me out. Christian probably suspected I was thinking of an exit plan. And as there's no better time to get out than when you're profitable, moving to a cheaper location was the smart thing to do.

Michelle, on the other hand, didn't take the news quite so well. In the past, I'd chosen my moments carefully when speaking to Michelle about the business. After all, what happened in the business affected her life as much as mine. This time, however, I was bursting with nervous energy. We were in the grocery store, and it wasn't that long after I'd spoken to Christian. In my head, I'd made the decision already, and all I had to do was break the news.

"Michelle," I said, "how would you feel about moving away from the Bay Area?"

Michelle jerked the shopping cart to a halt and turned to face me, confused. "Move? Why would we move? All our friends and family are here. Your business is here."

"We need to move Bizness Apps out of the Bay Area. It's just so damn expensive here. We can't find the right people. We're not getting the same growth."

When she realized I was serious, her face hardened. "There must be another way," she said.

"I wish there was. Trust me. I've spent weeks thinking about this. You know I want the business to stay profitable, and I don't see that happening here long term."

"You know what this means, right? It's not just about me. It's your staff too. Sam, Stephen, Zach, their families."

"Look I know some people are going to be upset, but—"

"But you want what's best for the business." Michelle sighed. Deep down, she understood why I thought moving was the right thing to do. She'd listened to me rant about losing people to well-funded companies, watched me sweat over plateauing growth numbers, and seen me grow weary with Bay Area politics.

It didn't take away from her sacrifice, however. All of her family lived in the Bay Area. Their roots ran deep. It wouldn't be easy leaving that all behind for the sake of her boyfriend's business. But she did. And living in San Diego turned out to be awesome for both of us. Without the distraction of friends and family, we had more time for ourselves and each other. We did almost everything together, going out for sushi, exploring the city, hanging out at the beach. This time alone rarely happened in San Francisco, illustrating just how easy it is to lose perspective when you're deep inside the hive. Our relationship matured in San Diego, and so did we, which culminated in me proposing to Michelle on a San Diego beach.

Could this have happened in another city? Of course. Neither of us expected the move to have such a positive impact on our relationship. I'd chosen San Diego for three less romantic but still important business reasons. One, it's one of the six largest cities in the US, with all the amenities you might wish for, and yet is still one of the most affordable places to live. You would need around $4,900 in San Diego to maintain the same standard of living you get with $8,100 in San Francisco. Two, it has already fostered some hugely successful businesses such as Qualcomm and newer startups like Aira. There's a thriving startup scene supported by fantastic communities like Startup San Diego that cultivate collaboration over insular, win-at-all-costs ambition. That's not a value judgment, by the way—you need a little of both—but learning from each other beats sticking a *Trespassers Will Be Shot* sign above your door! Finally, relocating to San Diego meant we could become one of the best places to work. While we hadn't conquered Silicon Valley, we had flourished there and proved ourselves a serious contender in the global tech space. Now we could offer San Diego talent one of the best working environments and benefits packages. We might not have had the in-house restaurant, gym, or bar, but we did offer a huge office (10,000 square meters) with wall-to-wall ocean views (fun fact: ocean views are linked to better mental health). In San Diego, few companies could afford such prime real estate, and coupled with our other benefits, this made us one of the top five or ten places to work. We went from being an average place to work in San Francisco to one of the best in San Diego.

How did the move impact our business? The numbers speak for themselves. We hired two world-class VPs we'd struggled to attract in San Francisco. Our operational costs fell 14 percent. Employee rent fell 37 percent on average, and commutes dropped to under thirty minutes. Our profitability soared 21 percent. We gained a lot of media attention and even had the mayor of San Diego open our new offices. We went from being the runt of the town to the talk of the town.

The Mayor of San Diego popped in to welcome us to our new office.

That said, there were drawbacks to the move I didn't fully realize until later. I put this down to naivete. Although I'd already moved the company once, from Chico to San Francisco, things were different back then. In people's eyes, San Francisco was an upgrade, so moving away felt like a failure to some. Even with a generous bonus and relocation package, some people felt hurt and let down, like we were abandoning them.

When you ask people to move 500 miles away, disparaging their home city isn't the best way to go about it. I'd forgotten how attached people get to places. They had friends and family in San Francisco. Some believed it was the best and only place to be if you were serious about a career in tech. I assumed the move would benefit everyone, but no one wants to be uprooted and replanted miles away from their loved ones. Despite my good intentions, I hadn't put myself in their shoes.

Before the move, I gathered feedback through employee surveys. Instead, I should've met with everyone individually, where I could have listened to their reservations and then helped them understand why the move would benefit them in the long run. I failed as a leader here and lost the trust of employees who felt undervalued by my decision. While it could've been a lot worse, in the end we lost about 7 percent of our employees. Nevertheless, I was committed to moving and soaked up the heat that came with it. I only wish I'd communicated things better to retain more of the people I'd become close to in San Francisco.

We did our best to make things easy on those who stayed behind, letting them work remotely while they looked for another job. This had its own advantages, such as the San Francisco team being able to train the new team in San Diego. Most of our engineering team was remote, so the transition wasn't as rocky as it might've been. Nevertheless, having a San Francisco presence during the transition spared a lot of headaches. I recommend you do the same if you ever move your business from one place to another. If nothing else, you've got a fallback if it doesn't work out in the new location.

As a base of operations, San Diego was stellar. After the stress of the move calmed down, I focused the team on sustainable growth. We had our prime office location. We had reduced our expenses. We were in a city conducive to entrepreneurship, had the pick of local and international talent, and would spend the next few years honing our business model, scoring big partnerships and more press and putting money in the bank.

But a shadow fell over the business in 2016 when Apple changed its developer guidelines. The rug was about to be pulled from under my feet with no warning, no time to prepare or strike back. Our business model was on course for redundancy. How could I bring it back from the brink?

CHAPTER 7

THE SAN DIEGO YEARS

Refining Focus, Redefining Motivation, and Other Challenges

WAS MOVING TO SAN DIEGO THE PANACEA TO MY exhaustion, the dizziness of a multiyear slog to get the business off the ground? It was certainly one of my best decisions as CEO and, ultimately, as an entrepreneur. I had a bit more time to think, to reflect on how I'd arrived at running a multimillion-dollar company I started in my dorm room. But this breathing space also made me realize I wasn't just fatigued. I was ready to move on.

Being a CEO is hard. It's a lonely, lonely role. You're in charge of everything—from getting snacks in the office to making sure everyone has what they need to succeed. You don't get to talk about it much. You can't walk up to your sales team and say, "Hey, I'm feeling a bit stressed out about our revenue goals." You have to keep that stuff inside and instead motivate them, give them ideas, and get in the trenches alongside them to close the gap.

You can't talk to your parents or friends, either. How would they relate? "Hey, Andrew! How was your day?" they'd ask, and I'd say, "Oh, you know, there's a customer that's really bothering me. A new competitor is coming to the market, and I'm concerned about our product. Also, the software has bugs, and customers are really upset. I'm also not sure if our new marketing strategy guy is working out. Also, our servers have been crashing a lot lately. How was your day?"

I bore the emotional weight of over a hundred people on my shoulders, and let me tell you, that pressure gets to you. You never feel quite good enough. Everyone's looking at you to build this extraordinary company, expecting you to have all the answers, and of course you never do. But when things go wrong, you're first in line for interrogation. As CEO, I was in charge of strategy, hiring, and results. And if those I'd appointed to these roles failed, it was also *my* failure, as I'd hired them. If it wasn't for my wife Michelle, the secret co-founder of Bizness Apps, and Christian, who was the best mentor I could have wished for, I think I'd have gone mad.

So after sailing Bizness Apps through a few early storms to arrive safely in the port of San Diego, I got cold feet. I'd learned so much in just under a decade that I began wondering what would happen if I applied my experience to a new business. Of course, they were just fleeting thoughts back then, but I knew that I'd risen several ranks as an entrepreneur through the most rigorous initiation rite you could possibly imagine. And the biggest test was yet to come.

OUR FIGHT WITH APPLE

You never know when your nemesis will appear or what form it will take. It might be a competitor, a market shift, or a new technology, or it could simply be a third-party decision that turns your world upside down. At our peak, we had tens of thousands of iOS apps on the App Store. Restaurants, schools, bars, gyms, hotels, designers, artists—you name a small business, and we made an app for it. And who wouldn't want their business on the world's number-one app marketplace, servicing the world's number-one smartphone?

In 2017, Apple changed their developer guidelines, rejecting every app we'd ever made. By doing so, they removed an important marketing medium from hundreds of thousands of small businesses across the world—those that couldn't afford the $100,000 to build an app from scratch.

See, we weren't in the *app building* business. We were in the *helping small businesses* business. Many of our customers were family businesses and sole traders that didn't have the deep pockets of Starbucks or Amazon. Worse, Apple cleaned out *every* app—even those that had won design awards—plunging our customers and our customers' customers into the dark.

When I got the call that all our apps had been rejected, I was despondent. How could we possibly fight this?

It was the first time in years that I felt helpless. I'd worked so hard to help small businesses succeed, and now everything had been undone in a sweeping change of Apple policy. The *why* behind Apple's decision mattered far less than knowing if Bizness Apps would survive the change.

Worse, Bizness Apps was one of the first that Apple banned, leaving our competitors to continue offering their services unhindered. I'll be frank: this enraged me. Why had my business and customers been singled out? Why had our legs been cut from under us while others could swagger forward? I suppose being a leader in the industry put a big, shiny target on our back.

As long as our competitors weren't immediately affected, many of them didn't care about the long-term effects and wanted to look away. I remember speaking to the founder of one of these companies. Instead of facing the stark reality of Apple's decision, they suggested our business had it coming. They said that Apple must've had a legitimate reason to ban Bizness Apps while leaving others alone.

"Listen," I said, doing my best to be calm yet assertive. "This isn't about you and me. It's affecting our whole industry. You'd better start preparing now; otherwise, you're going to be in trouble later on too. I'm only telling you this because I care about the future of this industry and its customers. We were hit first because we're the biggest, but that ax is going to keep on swinging. So figure out your next move before it's too late."

My employees demanded answers too. They wanted to know whether the company could survive without Apple and whether they still had jobs. I said we'd fight it, but I couldn't immediately see our way out. Some left the business, thinking we were done. Others rallied around me, offering their ideas and support. Loyalty, when earned, is priceless.

Then the customer calls began—hundreds of them, every day, demanding to know when we'd publish their apps. I handled most of these calls personally, some of them late at night, soaking up the negativity like a sponge. Michelle brought me coffee while I sat in the spare room with the phone cradled in my neck, clicking through emails, contracts, and legal resources. Afterward, she sat next to me and listened to my battle plan. She pointed out weaknesses and suggested how I might better handle things.

I hope, reader, that you have a person like Michelle in your life if you ever encounter a challenge of this magnitude. It's not the kind of thing you can face alone. I'm not an emotional guy most of the time, but this fight with Apple brewed an unholy cocktail of emotions in me: rage, fear, depression. You name it, I felt it as keenly as a knife between the ribs. Michelle, however, cut through the noise and got me thinking clearly and sensibly about the problem.

"You're focusing too much on Apple when you should be thinking of your customers," she said. And she was right. Having been caught off guard, I'd misread Apple's move as an attack, so my instinct was to defend. Like I said, it was an emotional time. The real challenge, however, was how I could appeal Apple's decision while continuing to help our customers.

Immediately, I put in a request for an extension so we could at least keep our business moving forward while we formulated our appeal. I also got our engineers working on a progressive web app builder that would allow our customers to build applications that ran through their customers' browsers. Progressive web apps look and feel like a native app but are faster, lighter, and more reliable, as they don't require a download from the App Store. If Apple didn't back down, we'd pivot to progressive web apps as our plan B.

With a three-month extension agreed upon, I began reaching out to my press contacts. I emailed an overview of the situation to a senior reporter at *TechCrunch*. She called me almost immediately, and we discussed how Apple's decision was going to impact thousands of small businesses. I was the first to deliver the news, and the reporter published an article the next day that caught the attention of the entire tech community. The message was simple: this change in App Store policy would have potentially devastating effects on the millions of small businesses that relied on services like ours. To capitalize on the article's momentum, we created an online petition where a senior executive at Apple would receive an email every time someone added their name and opinion. We got over 4,000 signatures.

Our big moment came when I shared an app with Tim Cook that helped prevent teen suicide. It was featured on *The Today Show*, where Megyn Kelly discussed how the app helped students manage suicidal thoughts and the pressures of growing up (a touching moment for us to see our apps used in such a positive way). "Do these apps really not belong in the app store?" I wrote to Tim.

Yes, many of our customers didn't know how to develop apps, and some didn't care about the App Store either. They simply wanted to communicate with their customers in their customers' preferred medium. Our customers paid us to develop for them so they could focus on running their business, the same way they might hire an accountant to do their bookkeeping. Without us, these businesses, many of which were family run, would have to pay developers tens of thousands of dollars to build an app from scratch, or they'd have to do it themselves by learning to code Swift (the iOS app programming language).

I argued back and forth with the executive team. I gave them some options, such as excluding us from the App Store categories, exempting us from the changes, approving apps based on quality, and so on. In the meantime, a lobbyist firm invited us to join a coalition that was taking the issue to congress. *The New York Times* sent over a list of questions, and *The Today Show* even reached out for a comment.

At this point, we could've gone full tilt into a PR war, but my gut told me this was wrong. Even if we'd won, it would've been a Pyrrhic victory. There *were* a lot of poor-quality apps in the App Store, the majority of which were built using software like ours. We didn't have much control over what our clients made, and in some cases, they didn't need an app. It was this uncomfortable truth that drove Apple's decision. But instead of raising standards, Apple banned everything.

After I begged the executive team for another extension to finish our progressive web app builder, I emailed Tim one final time. I explained what this change meant not just for our customers but for our customers' customers. "This has far-reaching implications," I wrote. "Our customers rely on us to give them an easy, affordable channel through which to connect with their community. If we sever this connection, the community loses out just as much as the businesses."

The next day I got three phone calls: one from the app review team, one from an executive, and another from one of the managers of the App Store.

The first person called and said, "I hear you're looking for another extension. We're not doing those right now, but we can make an exception for you."

Were they still trying to fob us off?

I emailed again. "Hey, we're going out of business and need your help. What can we do to make this right by you and the millions of customers that rely on us?"

Though I didn't know it at the time, Apple was already thinking of ways to help us. We had a powerful story, an underdog story, the same story we'd been telling for years. I think Apple understood it made sense to be on the right side of that, which reinforces just how powerful stories can be.

An Apple executive called me an hour or so after receiving my email.

"Hi, Andrew. Before I say anything, I just want to let you know that this is highly confidential. Can you keep this between us for the moment?"

"Yeah. Go on."

"There's going to be a change to the 4.2.6 guideline."

Apple would accommodate app builders on two conditions. One, they must all be uploaded to a single developer account. And two, they must undergo rigorous quality testing before deployment. I then received a call from the App Store team, who said they were granting us a ninety-day extension to give us time to comply with the revised guidelines. At that point, the nightmare was over.

Negotiating with a giant like Apple was never going to be easy. But like everything else, you lean into the headwind and don't stop until you emerge on the other side of the storm. Bizness Apps had helped propagate iOS apps, putting them in the hands of millions of people. This was a good thing for Apple, and I was delighted they realized that in the end.

I'm also proud to have gone through it and come out having lost little. Our progressive web app builder proved very popular, an antidote to app fatigue in the years following the iPhone's launch. The change in Apple policy pushed us to think of mobile app development in a different light, improve our product, and approach our target market in new ways. Despite the stress and sleepless nights, the toughest challenges can make you a better entrepreneur. Of course, when you're knee-deep in the shit, it's not easy to see the bright side. But as long as you think of your customers, you seldom make a misstep.

Of course, if it weren't for my amazing team, the Apple debacle might've proved our undoing. Thankfully, I'd made it a priority to focus and motivate my teams long before the developer guidelines changed. One of my favorite coaches,

Phil Jackson, who led amazing teams like the dynasty Chicago Bulls and the LA Lakers, had a philosophy that no one person is better than the whole team. He focused everyone on the team's goals, explained how each player contributed, and got everyone communicating to get the job done. This idea of focus is vital to business and gave everyone at Bizness Apps the steady hands to withstand any crisis, including the Apple one.

CAN'T STOP THIS TRAIN: FOCUS AND MOTIVATION

Moving to San Diego had already shaken my team. It had forced them to leave friends and family for a city many had never even visited. Then the Apple fight knocked the wind out of us. Any other business might've given up or lost its best employees and customers. Not us. We continued to grow, stack profits, and turn down investment offers. How did we do it?

From the moment I began hiring teams, I knew it was important to have everyone moving in the same direction while finding fulfillment in their work. Happy, motivated teams are the lifeblood of any organization. They can work magic under extreme circumstances, even the Apple nightmare. This doesn't happen overnight, though. I learned how to create focused, motivated teams incrementally by listening to our customers and employees.

It started with our roadmap. There was always so much to do, and we had to decide when and how to do it. Should we launch a new feature? Should we hire this person or start this marketing campaign? When you try to do too much in one quarter, you lose focus, and when you lose focus, you lose efficiency. In our early years, we tried to be everything to everyone. And when you're talking to everyone, you're essentially talking to no one.

In the years leading up to the Apple crisis, we started focusing on certain industries, like restaurants, automotive, schools, or anything with a loyalty program (hair salons, for example). We refined our roadmap to reflect the key industries in which we'd have the most impact. In the early days, you have lots of different customers, and your job is to figure out which ones provide the most value, which is usually those whom your business helps most.

Now once you identify your best customers and their qualities, it's a million times easier to market to them. The more you know about your customers, the more you can tailor their experience. You can personalize everything from advertisements to emails to user experience design. Your engineers know what to build. Your customer support teams know who to prioritize. Your salespeople know who to call. Teams work harder when they know what to do but even more so when they know how their actions affect the business's performance.

After the Apple crisis, we categorized our resellers too. Some were one-man bands with two or three clients, while others had twenty to fifty. These were the resellers we focused on. The benefit of spending most of your energy on key customers is they end up loving you more for thinking specifically about their needs. You can also be tougher on those that don't fit. If someone doesn't like the product and is difficult to deal with, you can politely say, "Perhaps we're not the right fit for you," confident you already know the answer and won't lose much if they walk.

However, if I wanted a team that was both agile and resilient to external forces, focus alone wouldn't be enough. I also needed to motivate them. If focus sets the ship's direction, motivation is the wind in its sails. We had goals to hit, but how could we make those goals come alive? No one wants to break their back working for a number.

One way we tackled this was by fostering competition within the business. Each team (we called them pods) would compete for a chance to go out for a steak dinner. All of it was lighthearted and fun. We'd always switch up the pods so everyone got a win. We'd also do regular work outings. One year, I took the whole company to the Del Mar horse races on a big bus with music, drinks, and snacks for everyone. We also booked entire restaurants and invited everyone and their families for parties. That's how you get that extra 20 percent out of people. You create the right culture, ensure they enjoy what they do, give them realistic goals and all the help they need to accomplish them, and then reward them regularly so they never lose momentum.

Hanging out with the team was always so much fun.

You're only ever as fast as your slowest team member, so you need to make sure everyone has the support they need to excel. Pressure and frustration impede performance. You need to explain how everything works, how each department connects, and how that combines to make happy customers. When attending my 10X CEO coaching sessions, all we talked about was how to create high-performance organizations. I always used to say, "If I'm going to build a company, I want to build one I'd like to work at." For me, that was making work fun. I wanted them to love their jobs, to feel valued and understood. If anyone seemed a little down or demotivated, I'd say, "Hey, you okay? Why don't you take the day off and rest? We'll see you tomorrow."

One of many rooftop happy hours.

It takes a team to win. No single individual can carry the weight of the organization (I tried that once and it almost killed me!). But harmony isn't won; it's fought for. Every day, I encountered new problems. An employee might be unhappy. Someone might want to quit. A customer might have complained, and so on. Once you put out one fire, others appear. But it was my job to communicate and contextualize employees' goals, as well as clear the path to their accomplishments. When your employees know you have their back, they're more productive, and you get closer to that high-performance culture.

I've seen what happens when a company lacks focus, accountability, and clearly defined goals. People diverge and burn out. They turn on one another. If you want to be a great place to work, ensure every employee knows what success looks like, and give them everything they need to achieve it.

We'd reached an agreement with Apple. Our business was growing profitably. I'd matured as a person and as an entrepreneur. What was next? San Diego was working well for us. I had no intention to move. But something was missing. I felt different, like I'd plateaued. I didn't want to chair a board. I didn't want to cede control of the business to a VC firm. The truth is, I was reconfiguring my priorities. I was only twenty-nine. I'd built a multimillion-dollar company from a $50,000 investment, and as proud as I was, I was ready for something new.

I'd had many acquisition offers for Bizness Apps. And why not? It was a profitable, growing SaaS business with an excellent reputation, millions of happy customers, and some of the best talent in the world. We were an investor's dream. So why hadn't I sold? With millions of dollars dangling in front of you, it's very tempting, but money has never really motivated me. What got me out of bed was helping people, delighting customers, and making my employees happy. This, I think, is what made the company so successful in the first place.

So why did I sell Bizness Apps? How did it happen? What made the process so difficult yet rewarding?

CHAPTER 8

END OF AN ERA AND BEYOND

EMERGING FROM THE APPLE CRISIS, bruised but still standing, I took stock of the business I'd spent eight years building. I started Bizness Apps while still in college and spent most of my youth working 100-hour weeks to build it into a company that generated $10 million in annual recurring revenue. It was my first serious company, and I embraced leadership without any prior training or experience. Of course, I stumbled, but that willingness to stumble is what made Bizness Apps possible in the first place.

That said, eight years is a lifetime in startup terms. It was apparent to everyone that Bizness Apps was never going to go public. We might've continued down the profitability route, but those returns would diminish over time too. The longer you focus on profitability, the more you realize it's all about reducing expenses and reinvesting every spare cent in growth.

Eventually, you might cut spending where it matters, leaving you with an inferior product or service, and then bleed market share to your competitors.

Selling, therefore, was on everyone's mind: mine, my investors', and even my senior management team's. It was the perfect time. We'd gone from almost losing the business to being back on top again. Everyone was ready to say goodbye.

LETTING GO

Every founder wants to sell. Building a business is an investment, and selling is when all your time and energy finally return a life-changing check. I'm sure you've thought about it once or twice, even if you don't own a business—daydreaming about being the boss, walking away with a few million dollars, and starting a new life free of the financial worries so many people bear. I knew I wanted to sell Bizness Apps the moment I founded it. It was simply a matter of when.

In 2016, I had hired an investment bank to put out the word that Bizness Apps was entertaining offers. I'd already built relationships with too many PE firms to count, as well as strategic acquirers including GoDaddy, Web.com, Deluxe, J2 Global, and Endurance International.

I did get a couple of offers, but neither one amounted to anything. One wanted the whole team to move to Florida, and I didn't want to inflict yet another big move on my staff. They also wanted a big earnout, which meant the price was contingent on the performance of the business after the sale.

I didn't think that was fair since I'd have very little control over performance after leaving the business.

The other offer was a 70 percent buyout from the well-known private equity firm Private Equity Partners, but it fell through. Again, I just didn't feel the terms were right, and as Bizness Apps was still growing, I thought I'd stay on a little longer. Then the Apple issue came along, and I kicked myself for not getting out when I had the chance. Luckily enough, two years later, I managed to sell Bizness Apps at the same valuation. Even without the Apple issue, a lot could have changed in two years, and I was fortunate to still command the same valuation.

Finally, one day I received a call out of the blue from an associate of ESW Capital, an acquisition firm that buys software businesses. I was fresh off the Apple fight and in dire need of a good night's sleep. They asked me if I wanted to sell. I said, "Sure. Who are you guys? I'm always up for entertaining an offer if that's what you guys do."

When they sent their offer, I couldn't believe it. I was able to negotiate a full stock purchase rather than an asset purchase, which meant tax liabilities were low. Better yet, they were also willing to buy the $2 million cash we had in the company account. Normally, buyers don't want to buy the cash in an acquired business since it just adds to the purchase price. Instead, they distribute it to equity-holders as a dividend, but with higher tax liability. Since ESW included it in the acquisition, we paid less tax, making it an incredibly favorable deal. They let me leave quickly, cards on the table, with an amount that meant never worrying about money again. I thought it was too good to be true, but ESW had a strong track record of fulfilling their promises, with a 98 percent[7] close rate on their letters of intent (LOIs), which is the first "official" offer from a buyer before the final deal is settled.

As you've probably guessed, I accepted. With an offer like that on the table, how could I refuse? I'd probably have sold the company for half as much. Nevertheless, I tried to be as cool as possible when ESW Capital got in touch. I didn't know much about acquisitions before this point. Usually, founders value their business as a multiple applied to revenue using a precise mathematical formula. Buyers want to see proof of the multiple's legitimacy in your financial metrics. I had a figure in mind but had no idea what was going through the mind of ESW Capital at the time.

While I was astonished by their purchase, this type of "founder-friendly" offer is actually quite common. A PE firm will have a team that goes after valuable SaaS startups, offers to buy them on great terms, and then takes over the companies and continues operations. This way, they acquire companies with superior growth and profitability potential quickly, without lengthy negotiations or founders inviting other buyers to the table. ESW Capital was a $10 billion fund, and they'd acquired hundreds of businesses, so they were a slick outfit.

I barely ate or slept for the next thirty days. I knew the buyer could pull out at any moment, for any reason, so I

---

7   "ESW Capital Overview," ESW Capital, accessed October 25, 2020, http://www.eswcapital.com/wp-content/uploads/ESW-Capital-Overview.pdf (content removed).

answered every due diligence request as fast as possible. I hired the best law firm too. Once I understood this acquisition was going to happen, I didn't want to mess it up. Another ESW Capital might not come around again.

First, they gave me the LOI. Then, along with the stock purchase agreement, they gave me a long due diligence document that was to be completed in thirty days. If you've never done acquisition due diligence, I'd compare it to an audit— the most thorough audit you can imagine. They weren't just pulling apart the financials but the technology, operations, business model, and countless other things. It was enough work for me, my CFO, my VP of Product, and my VP of Engineering for a straight thirty days without stopping, at sixty hours per week.

As you might imagine, our "secret project" raised a few eyebrows. I didn't want to cause any undue concern, so I told employees we were being audited by the Internal Revenue Service. This was close to the truth since potential buyers do audit the hell out of you to ensure your business is a good investment. We wrote a book on how to run our company, including everything about our server architecture, customer support operations, and marketing strategy, as well as every role, responsibility, and function of the company. ESW Capital went through our software and open-source libraries. We even had to rebuild certain features and remove specific open-source libraries we had used for years for legal reasons.

Not everyone was as excited about the potential change of ownership, however. I didn't know what would happen to my employees when I sold Bizness Apps, but I suspected some would lose their jobs. ESW Capital had a habit of reducing staff post-acquisition to increase profitability, and most acquisitions, especially financial ones like Bizness Apps, involved layoffs. I wish I could've offered my employees some guarantees, but there are no guarantees until the buyer wires the money. Only then is a business 100 percent sold. I didn't want people panicking over nothing.

I told employees on a Friday, which I expected to be closing day, when everybody would sign the stock agreements and the buyer would send out wires to investors, me, and everyone with equity in the company. The atmosphere was charged. Some employees looked up ESW Capital's past acquisitions online. People didn't know if they were getting fired or becoming millionaires. But then ESW Capital called to ask for an extra document from us before we could finalize the sale. Suddenly everyone was left in the dark. I had to tell people, "I don't know what's happening next, but there's a new owner coming in, and we're still working out the details." I'd hoped to avoid unnecessary panic, but it was starting anyway.

We had another false start the following Tuesday and didn't close the sale until Thursday. I formally announced the acquisition to the company and told them there would be a ninety-day transition period where I'd help the new owners meet everyone, get to know operations, and so on. But after that ninety days, I was out.

My first priority, however, was taking care of my employees. When you sell a business, you have zero control over what the new owners do. They could fire anyone, and you wouldn't even be consulted. It's like selling a house: you can't tell the new owners not to knock down a wall or change the wallpaper. They don't need your permission to do anything, and you'd be laughed out of the building if you expected it.

Since I couldn't guarantee my employees job security, the best I could do was ensure they profited from the acquisition. I gave everyone the option to leave with a generous severance package and helped them find new jobs. On top of that, ESW had given me a check for $500,000 to seed a new business. I decided instead to share the money equally with my team members. Many had already received lump sums from their stock options, so this was a bit extra in their pockets.

AFTERSHOCKS

When that wire transfer hits your account, it's a moment you never forget. I was in shock. I was worried that I'd made a mistake, that the buyer was going to call me up and say, "This isn't what you said it was!" and then hurl a lawsuit in my face. Of course, everything was fine, and they didn't find anything wrong. But when you've just been given millions of dollars for something you started in your student dorm room, your mind plays tricks on you!

You might be wondering what a twenty-nine-year-old did with all that money. Well, I did my best to put it to good use. Having lived in small, dated accommodations for most of my life, I wanted to give my family a home they'd be proud of.

So I bought Michelle and I a house in San Mateo where we could raise children (our first child treats it like a giant jungle gym). My parents still live in San Clemente, but when they're ready to move, they'll have their own house waiting for them too. I did splurge a bit on a C63 AMG Mercedes, but it was the first time I'd treated myself in a very long time, so I don't feel too guilty about it.

The rest is all in the stock market or seeding new business ideas. Not the mad spending spree you were expecting? I think Sir Thomas Mallory sums it up nicely: "Enough is as good as a feast." Wealth's most powerful and profound effect, in my experience, is the freedom to pursue your passions and provide for your family. Everything else is just a bonus.

In hindsight, however, I should've spoken to multiple buyers to perhaps get a better price. That's not to say ESW Capital's offer wasn't good—it was—but it's standard practice to shop around first and not accept the first offer you get. Otherwise, you might get swept away by the offer itself without knowing if it's a fair reflection of your company's value.

I always believed acquisitions involved the buyer falling in love with your company and offering you this big, round number. You know, something like, "Hey, your business is growing and profitable. I'll give you $50 million for it." But it's math-driven, which isn't my strong suit. When companies sell, they sell for numbers to two or three decimal places. It's not "10x revenue" but a sophisticated formula derived from your current and projected metrics. In that sense, not all buyers will come to the same figure, which is why it's useful to get a few offers in first.

That said, I was (and still am) more than happy with the offer I got from ESW Capital. And I feel very fortunate to have gotten out of Bizness Apps when I did. You never know when some crazy obstacle is going to collide with your business (such as the Apple issue) or if some bigger, leveraged party is going to copy your business model and do it better than you. Only last year, in 2020, Amazon released HoneyCode, a mobile app builder powered by AWS, the same server architecture that powers most of the internet. With that kind of digital footprint, there was little Bizness Apps could've done to fend off an attack on its market share.

Selling Bizness Apps closed a long chapter of my entrepreneurial career and life in general. Michelle and I got married a month before the sale was completed, so you can imagine how stressful that period was, trying to organize a wedding while finalizing the sale of a multimillion-dollar business. But, of course, it's a lucky problem to have. I remember someone at ESW Capital saying, "Wow, good for you. You just got married, and you're selling a company. You're kicking off being a husband really well." It was a proud moment.

There's no formal job training for entrepreneurship. Bizness Apps probably would have been about five times bigger had I known then what I know now. There's so much I would do differently. I'd hire better talent earlier, focus on customer success straight out of the stalls, and invest more in growth to capture market share faster. But that's what entrepreneurship is all about. It's about learning through doing, being passionate, and believing in your mission. I had all that in spades and still do, and for my next businesses, I have a few tricks up my sleeve, having already built and sold my first profitable startup.

WHAT NEXT?

True entrepreneurialism is *serial* entrepreneurialism. Don't get me wrong—I understand that some people happily run the same business for their entire lives. There's nothing wrong with that. But that wasn't for me. I wanted to keep pushing myself, even in areas that were new to me, to help others avoid the mistakes I'd made. And after my days of running Bizness Apps, I still had a general itch to see where I could help people achieve success in their lives and livelihoods.

Oh, and every year, starting a business becomes easier. Even for those with zero technical expertise, with a little vision, you can go far.

In my final years at Bizness Apps, I'd begun working on a new business called Altcoin that helped people trade cryptocurrencies. You'd think blockchain engineering would be above the skillset of a nontechnical founder, but that didn't faze me a bit. I could see the industry had yet to mature, but hundreds of millions of dollars' worth of blockchain-issued assets (bitcoin and ethereum, for example) were being traded every day.

I won't replicate Altcoin's entire story here, but it's worth mentioning the potential for disruption in capital markets, especially illiquid markets like fine art and property. Imagine a Monet going up for auction with a million digital tokens representing a share of ownership—all of which can be traded, transferred, and redeemed, leaving an indelible transaction record. You could democratize capital markets, fractionalize assets to boost liquidity, and underwrite every transaction with blockchain certainty. That was a big opportunity, and I could see my opening: most of these digital assets were traded on centralized exchanges that were often hacked to the tune of millions of dollars. I immediately thought, *Why isn't there a safer way to trade?*

After some research, I discovered there *were* alternatives to storing your digital assets on a centralized exchange, but they were slow and expensive and had terrible user experience design. They were built for tech-minded people, not the general public. I decided to build a platform that didn't store assets but instead let traders exchange them from their private wallets (virtual repositories protected by the owner's private key). It wasn't a revolutionary idea, and there were iterations of it in the market, but my idea was to go a step further and create something fast, secure, *and* easy to use, which didn't exist at the time.

But was there a business in this? Had I really hit upon something novel? Was the right technology too far away? To answer these questions, I hired a remote engineering team to build an MVP to get some feedback from the market. In the meantime, I formulated the story that would propel the project forward, just as I'd done at Bizness Apps. I had a three-step plan: first, capture the scale and potential of blockchain-issued assets. Then, posit the problem of centralization standing in its way. Finally, present Altcoin as the solution.

This is the kind of disruption that got me excited about blockchain. Capital markets are worth trillions of dollars. With that kind of money at stake, you need to ensure those trading digital shares of six-star hotels or famous sculptures have a safe place to do so. And Altcoin was the answer. Altcoin's mission was to empower people to access and then leverage a new, potentially profitable era of finance.

In just four months, the team and I set several technological milestones. We completed the world's first bitcoin-to-ethereum atomic swap (a kind of simultaneous exchange of assets without the assistance of a third party) and developed layer-two scaling solutions (techniques that increased the speed of blockchain transactions) using plasma and state channels. We released several betas of our decentralized digital-asset exchange to thousands of people to near-universal acclaim and hired our first executive, Ken Kavanaugh, to help sell our technology to other companies.

While Altcoin opened up exciting possibilities, I knew I wouldn't stick with it forever. Serial entrepreneurship is a continuous struggle to make the world a better place. You don't stop after solving one problem—you move on to the next.

The following month, Simon Dixon, CEO of BnkToTheFuture, an online investment platform, approached us with an acquisition offer. He wanted to launch a decentralized security token exchange (which they did in 2020), and our technology helped cut their time to market. While I could've continued working on Altcoin, there were legal challenges to operating in the digital currency space, and traditional financial institutions didn't want anything to do with us. Had we been a bit larger, I might've fought back, but our strength was in our technology. We couldn't afford a legal fight with the global banking system. Instead, I passed the baton to Simon and BnkToTheFuture as they were already an established player and could take Altcoin across the finish line.

I'd invested some of my own money to get Altcoin off the ground. Not a fortune by any standards. Just enough to hire some talented people to help make my vision for the company a reality. Later, I also raised around $800,000 through a WeFunder campaign, which was testament to a generous and supportive community that believed in our mission. We had yet to achieve our goals when Simon made his offer, but we delivered a working, efficient model and let the talented engineers at BnkToTheFuture finish the job. It was the right move for me, as I was a little over my head at the time, and in retrospect, the industry was still too young.

The important thing is that I saw a problem, built a solution, and then sold that solution to another company with the weight to push things further. This again proves you don't need millions of dollars to start a business. You just need the right idea and attitude.

With Altcoin sold off in June of 2019, I started consulting

for other companies, helping them improve their growth and revenue strategies. It's not something I set out to do, but people were contacting me all the time asking for help, and I was honored to oblige.

One of my goals was to help people avoid the problems I'd encountered with Bizness Apps. Perhaps my biggest achievement at that time was helping Spiff, a commission automation platform, grow 1,000 percent in just ten months and secure a $10 million series A investment. I'd met Jeron Paul, the founder, numerous times, and he was no rookie, having built and sold several businesses himself. Spiff's mission was simple but powerful: what if you could automate sales commission calculations? For salespeople, time is everything. So the easier you make their compensation plan, the happier and more motivated they become.

Jeron and I had coffee, and he asked if I'd be interested in joining his team, initially as a consultant. I said yes and within a few weeks was officially appointed Chief Revenue Officer. When I reviewed their sales process and marketing strategy, I noticed they were making the same mistakes I'd made at Bizness Apps, so my work involved deploying solutions to problems I'd already solved. It wasn't groundbreaking stuff—just the advantage of experience. After Norwest Venture Partners invested in Spiff's series A, I bowed out, thanking Jeron for the opportunity to focus on another new business.

All the while, I was still reflecting on my experience of selling Bizness Apps. Even though it was a dream turning point in my life, the process was incredibly stressful and lacked clarity. I wondered, *Was all that turmoil necessary, and could it have been done better?*

I can tell you firsthand, acquisitions can turn even the most resilient founder into a nervous wreck. First, there's the question of whether or not to sell. Then it's wondering if it's the right price. Finally, it's dealing with the push and pull of due diligence, exit negotiations, false starts, disgruntled employees, and so on before the wire finally lands in your account and you're on to something new. For some, the acquisition process is so daunting they put off selling at all. I mean, hiring investment banks and lawyers is a costly exercise, and you never know if an acquisition will go through until it does.

Naturally, when founders meet, they discuss these things— they want to know how others handled it. This got me thinking about whether there was a better way to buy and sell companies.

Hear me out: what if acquisitions were more like dating apps? You advertise your startup with its key metrics, and buyers can contact you for more information. You wouldn't need to hire an investment bank. You wouldn't pay any fees or commissions. Would that help more entrepreneurs move on to the next phase of their careers? Would that prevent founders from holding out until it was too late and their career had stalled? Would it help buyers if they could filter businesses on pre-vetted metrics that mattered?

Startup marketplaces aren't new, but they're mostly small or specialized. I wanted to think a little bigger. What if anyone could sign up, buyer or seller, and get the info they needed to put an LOI on the table within thirty days?

Well, I hope by the time you read this I'll be further along with MicroAcquire and its mission of making acquisitions easy. Who knows? Perhaps I'll have built and sold it. Maybe I'll be CEO of the latest unicorn. Just kidding. For now, it's keeping me out of trouble. I'm a father now, and I'm spending more time with family and less time glued to my iPhone checking emails.

That said, MicroAcquire represents something very important to me. In a way, it brings my story full circle. I've always wanted to help people succeed. I've never felt it right or necessary to step on others to get where I am today. It's always been about looking at problems in a new light, asking questions, imagining how things would be different. Now that I've played the startup game and won several times, I want others to share in my success. I want them to learn from my experiences so they can build their own businesses and create their own solutions to the problems of our imperfect world.

MicroAcquire is yet another great leveler. With Bizness Apps, it was helping small businesses compete by making it cheaper and easier to build mobile apps. With MicroAcquire, it's about giving founders a platform for selling their business without the pain of intermediaries and hefty commissions. It's about democratizing acquisitions, celebrating small achievements, and opening up a world of opportunities for buyers and sellers alike.

I wrote earlier that my time at Bizness Apps—nine

years—was a lifetime in startup land. What would I have done had I advertised it on something like MicroAcquire? Would I have sold earlier? Would I already be on my third or fourth business, springboarding from one profitable acquisition to another? Would I have attracted more offers or *better* offers? I'd certainly have spent less and quite possibly have sold earlier and for a larger amount had I been able to advertise to buyers directly. Hindsight is a wonderful thing.

Building and selling profitable startups isn't easy, but it is simple. The basics of building a profitable business are the same today as they were thousands of years ago when the first chicken was bartered for a sack of rice. So I'd like to close this chapter by going back to the fundamentals I spoke about at the beginning.

WHAT IS TRUE ENTREPRENEURSHIP?

Know this: The belief that your startup needs to be original kills entrepreneurship. What's more important is that you solve a problem and solve it well. There are very few original ideas anymore, and to wait around for one to magically appear could take years. Why waste that time when you could go out into the world and see the gaps that need filling? What do people care about? What do they complain about? What do people love and hate? How do they do the things they do? What problems do they have? What can you make more efficient? Easier? More *fun*?

Become a student of human behavior, and you'll spawn a

thousand new business ideas. Once you understand people, you understand the world. Finding your niche is then easy, and it might even grow into a substantial wedge. It won't happen overnight, and you'll have to embrace failure if you're serious about entrepreneurship. Show me all the multimillion-dollar founders, and I bet you every one of them has climbed to the top upon piles of broken ladders. *If you're scared to fail, you're scared to succeed.*

Again, true entrepreneurship is *serial.* It's a journey where you learn from each successive venture until you're happy to put the brakes on. This might be when you're doing what you love. Perhaps you hit upon a business that you want to pass on to your children. Maybe it's when you have a string of profitable acquisitions under your belt (or even just one) and you're ready to retire or focus on more important things like friends and family. Don't get bogged down in one idea. Develop several, and hedge your bets. And keep learning. You'll find it a fulfilling and rewarding career, and you don't need venture capital to make a lot of money from it either.

The point here is that it can take multiple attempts to get your career going. I had PhoneFreelancer before Bizness Apps and a string of other businesses before then. I see a few more in my future too.

Finally, let's pause for a moment and talk about money. I'm guessing you're reading this because you're interested in building a business, or maybe you've built one already and are ready to sell. Whatever the reason, please allow me to caution you on money as motivation. If you're an investment banker, your desire to make money is an asset. It's certainly important in entrepreneurship, too, but in a different way. Making money is really just a byproduct of solving problems. I understand this sounds facetious, but stick with me a moment. I was never interested in money. I'm the guy my friends call "Simple Gaz." Flash, glitz, and ostentation were never my thing. Instead, I was interested in building businesses. Yes, they were profitable, but this was a means to an end. If we were profitable, that meant we could keep going, keep growing, keep helping our customers succeed. It was a symbol of doing things right.

I remember meeting lots of founders in our Silicon Valley days whose sole purpose appeared to be raising funding, as if a series A was some kind of badge of honor. They were pushing for that billion-dollar valuation. They slaved day and night for it, shackled to boards, private equity firms, and angel investors looking to multiply their ROI as quickly as possible. These people looked like hell. I felt sorry for them. They were slogging their guts out to boost their valuation and had lost track of what mattered.

Think about it: if you run a SaaS company on a subscription model, your revenue depends on how well your product serves your customers. Now you could think, *I need to find new routes to market, spend money on advertising, and hire more salespeople.* This might butter your bread for a while. But what if you took that thinking to a higher level? "How can I serve our customers even better so they tell more people about us, leave better reviews, and buy our upgrades?" It's a subtle difference, but in only one of these examples are you targeting what matters: customers. Please them, and everything else follows. If you're in entrepreneurship because you think there's easy money to be made, you're going to be disappointed. Entrepreneurship is *crazy* hard work. You'll fail countless times. People might hate your product or service. But that's okay. It's all part of the fun. You have to enjoy it. You need passion and a coat of armor. You need the commitment to see your ideas through and the courage to walk away when they fail. Resilience is an important quality in an entrepreneur, more so than a Harvard MBA or a $10 million investment. Stephen King admits to hundreds of rejections before his debut novel *Carrie* got published. It's the same with building businesses. You need to keep trying until you hit upon the one that works.

I hope my story has helped you. I know we haven't met, but I imagine we have a lot in common. You're either just starting out or midway through your entrepreneurial career, so in that sense we've shared many experiences. With this book, I wanted to give an honest account of the successes and failures of entrepreneurship, how they affected me emotionally and psychologically, and how I navigated those treacherous waters to get where I am today. It's been a whirlwind of a journey, and with MicroAcquire underway, I sense another exciting journey ahead. Perhaps I'll see your business listed there sometime!

Feel free to reach out to me anytime if you have any questions about the content in this book or if you just want to shoot the breeze over coffee.

This is Andrew Gazdecki, founder, father, and serial entrepreneur, signing off.

Best of luck with all your endeavors.

Andrew Gazdecki

RESOURCES ON ENTREPRENEURSHIP

CHAPTER 9

SHOULD ENTREPRENEURS THINK MORE LIKE ANGEL INVESTORS?

STARTING YOUR OWN COMPANY IS HARD. You can expect pain, frustration, setbacks, and tears along the way—and perhaps even failure. The wins make you feel unstoppable, and the downs make you feel like you'll never figure out a way forward.

Entrepreneurs often wax lyrical about their billion-dollar ideas. But since it's often reported that the majority of startups will fail, I started wondering if there was a better approach to building a successful company.

INCREASING YOUR CHANCES OF ENTREPRENEURIAL SUCCESS

While focus is important, it can blind us to other opportunities and often our own failures. When you become attached to a business you believe will change the world, you'll probably fight tooth and nail to keep it afloat.

But competition is fierce, and successful funding rounds don't always mean success in the market. You need to work out a plan to get where you want to be, whether that's a $10 million exit, a $100 million exit, an IPO, or some other specific goal.

An angel investor, for example, might invest around $25,000 to $100,000 per startup to achieve positive returns on a small portion of them. One 2017 study, "The American Angel," cited average angel investments ranging from $32,000 to $44,000, depending on the U.S. region. Likewise, with $100,000 capital, you could potentially start ten businesses with a budget of $10,000 each, build ten MVPs, and gather feedback on all of them to find the one that resonates with the market, which could get you one step closer to your goal.

So instead of piling lots of time, effort, and money into one idea, you could spread your capital across several businesses and hedge as an angel investor would.

ANGEL INVESTING VS. TRADITIONAL ENTREPRENEURSHIP

Like angel investing, the more companies you build, the greater the chance should be that one of them will become a life-changing return on your time and capital. Where an angel investor increases their portfolio to maximize returns, you, as an entrepreneur, could apply your talents to other business ideas to multiply your chances of success.

Angel investors generally make small bets on startups and help them get through those tough early stages of growing a business. They make a lot of these bets. "The American Angel" showed that angels with entrepreneurial experience have an average of twelve companies in their portfolio.

Out of those small bets, only a handful—a very small percentage of them—are likely to become really successful. For example, "The American Angel" found that the angels they studied had a positive return on about 11 percent of their investments.

The odds of investing in a successful startup may be similarly low for both angel investors and traditional entrepreneurs. However, an angel investor diversifies to minimize losses and increase returns, while a traditional entrepreneur often chooses not to.

Many of the entrepreneurs I meet spend years or even decades on one business. Not all of them will succeed. But if they adopt an angel investor mindset, there's a good chance they'll achieve their goals.

MULTIPLY AND CONQUER:
A NEW MODEL FOR ENTREPRENEURSHIP

In business, success can pay for failure many times over. If you build nine unsuccessful companies, for example, but your tenth one is a success, it's possible you'll recover everything you've lost.

It's important, therefore, not to get too attached to one idea, at least until you have some traction, such as finding product-market fit with paying customers. In the meantime, I believe one of the most important steps in this approach is to get an MVP to market so you can gather feedback by speaking to customers and investors. It's much more powerful when you can share your vision with a working prototype.

Becoming an Agile Entrepreneur

An angel investor views each investment in terms of risk. Yes, it could be a multibillion-dollar company, but it probably won't be. So they split their capital across several projects.

In the same way, an agile entrepreneur splits their time and energy between several ideas. Remove your emotional attachment to one project, and you'll start to see things objectively. If your business fails to impress mentors, investors and customers, close it down. Stick it on your resume, and move on to the next one.

Time is your most valuable asset. To become an agile entrepreneur, you can think of your business ideas like how an angel investor thinks of investment opportunities. Build a portfolio of startups, aiming for one of them to succeed. An angel investor could receive a small return on a few companies, so consider following that strategy by starting more companies over a shorter period of time.

Sumner Redstone, the billionaire media magnate, is credited with saying, "Great success is built on failure, frustration, even catastrophe." So don't be afraid of failure. Plan for it. Think more like an angel investor, and you can mitigate failure as you would any other risk.

CHAPTER 10

WHO NEEDS INVESTORS? WHY MANY STARTUPS SHOULD BOOTSTRAP INSTEAD

WITH 500 STARTUPS ACCELERATOR'S NEW CLASS introduction video and its notorious chant, you can't help but wonder if the current system for funding startups is really the best route to build lasting companies. Some even believe that the funding-centric mindset of startups in Silicon Valley is toxic.

I couldn't agree more, which is why other than receiving some modest help, we opted not to pursue investors for our company and decided to go it alone instead. I'm convinced that for a lot of startups (though certainly not all), choosing to bootstrap instead of searching out VC money is the better strategy for a number of reasons.

FOCUS ON PLEASING CUSTOMERS, NOT INVESTORS

When you don't have a lot of money, you're forced to turn to the funding source that rarely tolerates mistakes: customers. Specifically, you should focus on the product results in the creation of an MVP, a pared-down core offering that delivers a clear value to customers. And if all of your efforts are focused on designing a product that customers want, enjoy, or find useful, you've got a much better chance at success than someone who's focused on convincing investors that the business will be viable one day.

Skeptical? Companies like SquareSpace, WuFoo, Braintree, Lynda.com, 37 Signals, Campaign Monitor, Github, and many more were able to become successful without relying on traditional rounds of funding. And we built our company, Bizness Apps, from the ground up without any significant outside funding (and we not only turned out just fine; we were also profitable).

Now that's not to say that a business can't chase both customers and investors at the same time, as many successful companies have clearly done just that. But in my opinion, it can be harmful to worry about what investors think when you should be worried about customers, a much more sustainable and important funding source.

LIMITS SET USEFUL BOUNDARIES

Being broke is a wonderful system for cutting through the options and setting limits. It forces you to think creatively about how to get things done. So where many established or funded companies tend to throw money at a problem and explore all the possible avenues, a bootstrapped company will have to find the best way, and fast. This leads to a culture of problem-solving that almost every successful company has to some extent.

At Bizness Apps we learned this while working on our mobile food ordering system. We couldn't afford to develop both native and mobile web versions at the time, so we made the conscious decision to initially develop an HTML5 version that would work across all mobile devices.

URGENCY INSPIRES EFFICIENCY

When you've got money in the bank and know the bills will be paid for months to come, it's easy to spend late nights debating the company's choice of colors for the logo while more important matters tend to get left for the next day. The bootstrapped company, on the other hand, is grinding it out to produce a product that sells. A lack of funding has a way of making prioritizing tasks easier.

A core sense of urgency usually leads to the most critical tasks being handled first while less important matters are saved for later (as they should be anyway). The result is more prudent spending. The product is designed in a focused manner, and team members and resources are employed more wisely. Thus the business as a whole enjoys a great return on each dollar and hour spent.

Without a huge runway at Bizness Apps, we went above and beyond for our first paying clients. Even though our service was do-it-yourself, we bent over backward to help new customers set up their mobile apps for them, knowing we wouldn't have a second chance. The extra effort paid off. Not only did this help improve our product and convert users to paying customers faster, but we gained invaluable feedback along the way.

The decision saved months of time and thousands of dollars in development costs. Doing so not only got us to market faster and cheaper but allowed us to get user feedback sooner and improve the product.

ENFORCING DISCIPLINE AND ACCOUNTABILITY

There's no room to be loose with resources, design, or responsibilities in a bootstrapped company. A culture of discipline in many areas of the business tends to arise organically; otherwise, the company falls apart pretty quickly. Deadlines can't be allowed to slide far, if at all, and every member of the team must be held accountable for delivering their share.

It's the discipline of a well-run acrobatic family: everyone has a job to do and a mark to hit at a particular time and place, or everything else comes crashing down.

In any industry, maximizing returns from time and money spent is often the most basic central goal. In a bootstrapped company, it's woven into the fabric of the enterprise. At the end of the day, all entrepreneurs who hope to build something more than just a salable idea should ask themselves one fundamental question: do they really need funding?

CHAPTER 11

FIVE WAYS BOOTSTRAPPING CAN MAKE YOU A BETTER BUSINESS

EVERY STARTUP IS KEENLY AWARE OF HOW MUCH MONEY it has and, more importantly, how much money it doesn't have. For most startups, the goal is to score a big round of venture capital funding and then get out of fundraising mode and into the business of growing the company.

But even if you get a round of funding, it rarely ends there. More often than not, series A becomes series B; series B becomes series C, and so on. While you're out spending all day and all of your energy raising the next round of financing, it dawns on you: your business isn't about its mission anymore. Your business is now the business of seeking funding. Some would even suggest that bootstrapping is overrated and that the number-one skill of an entrepreneur is raising capital, but I couldn't disagree more.

Now don't get me wrong: countless successful businesses have been launched with the help of VC funding. But I'm writing this piece to share some of the surprising benefits of building your business without it.

1. CUSTOMERS ARE A MORE SUSTAINABLE SOURCE OF FUNDING

In my opinion, it all comes back to the customers and sustainability. Without investor funding, a company is forced to listen to customers as if they were the bosses. And let's face it: they are. In any successful company, they pay the bills. After all, it isn't Apple's investors who line up around the block for those pretty new iPhones every season (although I'd like to see that).

Raising money from your customers also forces you to build a product that's not only desirable but that people will actually pay for. If you don't care to hear me preach, listen to patent junkie Thomas Edison, who said, "I never perfected an invention that I did not think about in terms of the service it might give others...I find out what the world needs; then I proceed to invent."

Focusing on the customers helps you avoid what can be a destructive funding-centric mindset as described above. Some even advise that as soon as you close the first round, you should gear up for the second round. In my opinion, focusing on the customer and building profitable products is much more likely to lead to a sustainable business.

2. YOU BECOME MORE AGILE AND EFFICIENT

Going at it alone forces you to use capital extremely efficiently, which creates a strong culture and builds a huge competitive advantage moving forward. This scrappy us-against-the-world approach is good, and it leads to a team of founders instead of employees. Not having millions to burn also makes you hungrier to find ways to improve organically, as opposed to attempting to spend your way out of problems and challenges.

As Paul Graham, co-founder of seed capital firm Y-Combinator, has said, "When you raise a lot of money, your company moves to the suburbs and has kids."

3. BUILDING ON A BUDGET CAN SOMETIMES BUILD A BETTER PRODUCT

Without a huge amount of funding in the bank, it's also much easier to pivot to a better product or strategy based on real paying-customer feedback.

Without funding, you're forced to find product-market fit through customer feedback, and at a much faster pace. You simply don't have the luxury of an eighteen-month burn rate, vacations included.

It's all or nothing, and the customers call the shots. Or, as Eric Ries, author of *The Startup Way* and founder of Lean Startup theory would put it, "Don't be in a rush to get big; be in a rush to have a great product."

4. YOU DON'T GIVE UP EQUITY IN RETURN FOR GROWTH

The economics of startups have fundamentally changed in the past few years, making it extremely easy to start a company on a shoestring budget. What used to take millions to build a few years ago can be done with a few thousand and a couple of cases of Red Bull today.

Sometimes all you need is a small seed round of financing to build an awesome MVP early users will pay for, helping to fuel additional product improvements. The key here is to find a specific demand in a large market and fill that void.

5. YOU CALL THE SHOTS AND REAP THE REWARDS

If you avoid VC funding, you have more control over everything from operational and financial policies to big items like your company's vision. When you agree to accept funding, on the other hand, you give up some control and become subject to potentially demanding investors who want to see returns.

As a result, your company can become much less flexible and nimble, as analysis and conservatism impede your decision-making and risk-taking. The ability to be inventive and take risks is supposed to be the main advantage of a startup, so don't be so eager to grow up that you miss out on your company's young, wild, and reckless years.

Even if you do need funding, as everybody knows, the best time to raise capital is when you don't actually need it (e.g., SquareSpace). It's like dating: those who don't seem to need a partner are often the most desirable. Seeking funding when you're desperate leads to bad terms and "take it or leave it" partnerships. Coming from a place of strength, in contrast, leads to desirable terms, valuation, and top-flight partners.

Moreover, if your goal is ultimately to sell the company, you can obtain a more favorable and profitable deal if you aren't subject to financing structures and didn't unload a chunk of the company early on (e.g., WuFoo).

In short, I think startups should place less focus on raising venture capital and more on their customers. At the end of the day, they're the ones who will help you build an awesome product and pay your bills.

RESOURCES ON GROWTH

CHAPTER 12

WANT TO GROW YOUR STARTUP? USE STORYTELLING TO SLAY THE COMPETITION

A GOOD BRAND STORY ELEVATES YOU ABOVE THE competition. While someone can copy your products or services, they can't copy your brand. So tell stories that excite your customers and align with their goals. Start movements around your brand. Only then, with a powerful story behind you, will you outshine your competitors—and perhaps lead your startup to a successful exit too.

STORIES ARE IN OUR BLOOD

Stories are how we make sense of the world. Our lives are full of beginnings, middles, and ends—some happy, some sad. Stories help us understand our role in a vast, dynamic world—one we can't assimilate through raw data alone. They're hard-coded in our genetics and our histories, making storytelling one of the most powerful influences on our thoughts and behavior.

Software company Salesforce, for example, is one of the world's leading customer relationship management (CRM) tools, which helps businesses communicate and build relationships with prospects and customers. But rather than focusing on customer management alone, their story begins with identifying a shift from on-premise software installations to the cloud. They went from saying, "You can manage your sales contacts with our tool," to "You don't have to install this on a computer. You can do this in the cloud and access your information from anywhere in the world, on any device." Sales teams could then access sales data when on the road or visiting clients, leaving them better equipped and with more time to do what they do best.

Salesforce was among the first to popularize the SaaS business model, which increased both the availability and flexibility of software. Once they identified the shift, they placed the responsibility of infrastructure on vendors, not consumers. This idea of flexible, scalable, available-anywhere software leveled the playing field for consumers. They didn't need expensive hardware anymore, just an internet connection. This was the happy ending customers wanted, and Salesforce gave it to them.

Describing what your product does isn't enough. Competitors will copy your business model. They might even do it better or cheaper than you can. When you compete on price, you're in a race to the bottom. But when you compete on brand, you're in a race to the top. You need to excite your customers, turn them into evangelists, and get them rooting for you, the hero of the story.

HOW TO TELL THE RIGHT STORY

So how do you tell a good brand story? Here is the framework that worked for me.

1. IDENTIFY A SHIFT

When I was in college, I noticed that every business wanted to market to their customers through mobile applications. This shift from desktop to mobile was the beginning of Bizness Apps's story.

2. CREATE A NEW CATEGORY

For the first time ever, Bizness Apps enabled small businesses to build mobile applications for less than the price of a newspaper ad. Finally, the little guy could stand up to bigger rivals and offer the same things: mobile ordering, mobile loyalty programs, push notifications, and so on.

3. REINFORCE A THEME

Some custom-built mobile apps can cost up to $200,000, so few of our prospects could afford a mobile strategy. To thwart their deep-pocketed competitors, our prospects needed access to the same tools, and Bizness Apps leveled the playing field by making those tools affordable.

4. START A MOVEMENT

Our movement was big business versus small business. By making custom mobile applications affordable, we helped small businesses compete. Our drag-and-drop mobile app builder probably wasn't the best in the market, but we told the best story.

BEST PRACTICE TIPS FOR STORYTELLING

Now that you've seen how powerful storytelling can be, and you have a framework to work with. What else can you do to ensure your story resonates with your customers?

First, keep your story simple. Maintain a sharp, lucid message throughout. It must be clear and easy to understand and told in your customers' language. Use visuals to reinforce your messaging.

Second, know your audience. Discover what your prospects and customers care about most. Take an MVP to market, and ask them for feedback. Stories work best when you elicit an emotion, so you must understand your buyers' needs, wants, and pain points.

Third, be consistent. Ensure that everyone in your business knows the story and that every channel you communicate through maintains the same message. Inconsistency breeds mistrust—a ruthless killer of any brand.

And finally, be personal. Add color and credibility to your story by including personal anecdotes people can relate to. Giving a little of your background humanizes both you and your brand. People buy from people, so your business should have personality.

Good stories spread like wildfire. Your customers will tell their friends and family. The press will write about you. And you'll be asked to tell your story on blogs, podcasts, and maybe even TV.

So if you want to rise above the competition in your field, start telling a story that matters to you, your industry, and your customers.

CHAPTER 13

HOW TO MAKE THE COMPETITION YOUR GREATEST ASSET IN SALES

ONE OF THE SIMPLEST WAYS TO START A BUSINESS IS to do what others do—but do it better. Not everyone has a killer idea, but a curious mind might ask, "Why don't we do it like this?" and then build a profitable business out of it. In fact, many businesses (think Amazon Echo and Google Home, Instagram Stories and Snapchat, Indiegogo and Kickstarter) have made millions by providing new solutions to old problems.

Later, however, this becomes a disadvantage. When you're successful, others will copy you. They'll look for the leaky timber in your hull. If you're not careful, they'll steal market share from under your nose, and there's very little you can do about it.

Or is there?

Competition does make sales tougher. But if you're strategic and focus on the right things in your business, you can actually use the competition to your advantage. It won't work miracles, but I guarantee you'll minimize customer losses *and* sharply define your proposition to carve out a bigger share of the market.

Here's how to turn your competition into your biggest asset.

BECOME WHAT'S MISSING

If you're improving on an existing product or service, you'll have researched the market to find who's doing the best job. It's then up to you to identify and plug any gaps, whether it's pricing, product, or customer service. But if you're introducing something new, you need to understand where it fits and who might copy you.

In both cases, the competition is a treasure trove of data. You can try their products, read their content, study customer reviews and testimonials, and talk to CEOs, founders, and other industry leaders. Seventy-eight percent of startups view networking, for example, as critical to their success.[8] It helps get a snapshot of the market: what's working, what's not, who's new, who's leaving, and so on. You might also meet your future customers.

What's important is you learn every inch of your competition. Then, you offer more than they do. Zero in on your

---

8   Federico Guerrini, "Study: For 78% of Startups, Networking
    Is Vital To Entrepreneurial Success," *Forbes*, November 10, 2016,
    https://www.forbes.com/sites/federicoguerrini/2016/11/10/
    study-for-78-of-startups-networking-is-the-key-to-entrepreneurial-success.

differentiators, and scream them from the rooftops. Well, not literally, but certainly build your brand story about what sets you apart. When customers need you most, the quality, timing, and relevance of your message can improve the perception of your brand[9], making a memorable experience for them. Sell your vision, not your products, since this is where you'll make your mark.

EMBRACE COMPETITION

Customers have all the data they need to make a buying decision at their fingertips. With 81 percent of Americans owning a smartphone,[10] they needn't rely on you to tell them what to buy. In fact, 88 percent of customers shop around, with 94 percent reading online reviews before making a purchase. The marketplace is crowded, but customers determine who gets picked.

You've got two responses to this. One, you hunker down on building a great product, telling the best story and delighting every customer who touches your business. Or you pick apart your competitors and use their weaknesses against them. I'll have more to say on the latter in a moment, but let me explain why the former is the right choice every time.

---

9   Sridhar Ramaswamy, "How Micro-Moments Are Changing the Rules," *Think With Google*, April 2015, https://www.thinkwithgoogle.com/marketing-strategies/app-and-mobile/how-micromoments-are-changing-rules.

10   "Mobile Fact Sheet," Pew Research Center, April 7, 2021, https://www.pewresearch.org/internet/fact-sheet/mobile.

Competition helps define your business. Like it or not, competition is a natural part of the marketplace, a feature of its landscape. Regulators break up monopolies for a reason: they're not good for business, and they're not good for customers. So embrace your competition, and let the qualities of your business speak for themselves.

Your sales messages don't exist in a vacuum. A prospect latches onto the closest appropriation of your offering to contextualize your offer. If you're pitching an online sales platform, for example, your customers immediately think of Amazon. If you're selling a new streaming service, they think of Netflix. So if you don't know how your business fits in, how can you possibly sell successfully?

Acknowledge competitors in your sales negotiations. Recommend customers speak to them or research their offerings. This might sound counterintuitive, but it creates trust and legitimacy. Nothing turns people off more than desperation. Customers will return if you're worth it, and trust could even be the deciding factor. And if not, you can find out why and use that to improve your business. Either outcome is a win.

STAY CLASSY

I wrote earlier that customers have the upper hand. A few taps on their smartphone, and they can bring up reviews and alternative vendors. I think the easiest way of dealing with this is to focus on your business, as outlined above.

But if you choose to focus on the weaknesses of your competitors, you're in dangerous territory. There's nothing against self-improvement through comparison; indeed, you can build businesses from that. But exposing those weaknesses to customers in a bid to win them over is *not cool.*

Badmouthing the competition makes you look weak, desperate, and sloppy. It seldom weakens their business but yours: how you behave toward others in your industry is one of the criteria by which potential partners and customers may judge you. While you might fool a few customers, the majority will see through the trash talk to the pettiness behind it. And once that bridge is burned, there's little you can do to rebuild it.

The competition is composed of people like you—hardworking teams who've dedicated their careers to making customers' lives better. Denigrating them doesn't make you look better; it makes you look bitter. Not just to customers, but to important people in the market: influencers, leaders, investors, and other people you will increasingly come into contact with and might one day rely on.

So no matter how bad the competition gets, no matter how crowded the market, don't attack your competitors. Stay classy instead.

INFLUENCER TACTICS

You're at the negotiating table. Your palms are sweaty. Your heart's racing. Close this deal, and you score a huge win for your business. But as you look into your prospect's eyes, you can see they're not giving in without a fight. They see tens of others like you every month, so why should they say yes to you? If what I've written so far has sunken in, you should be able to answer:

1. **You know you have something they want.** You've researched the market and dove deep into your competitors' propositions, and no one is offering what you are, for that price, for that feature set.

2. **You're going to let the competition speak for you.** You know who to mention, who to contrast yourself against to give your prospects an anchor and a frame of reference from which you'll persuasively explain, in the simplest terms, how you're better.

3. **You'll respect their current provider.** You have a reputation for respect and fair play. You'll acknowledge the strengths of their existing vendor while gently exposing how your offering surpasses theirs in ways your prospect cares about.

No matter how difficult the negotiation becomes, stay true to these principles, and you'll come out on top most of the time. People want value for money. You don't give that by ignoring or bashing the competition. You do it by offering an *engaging* product whose value is *self-evident* and *convincing*.

Without competition, these criteria are harder to prove—you might as well just send a brochure.

It's easy to fall into the trap of thinking competition is your worst enemy. But as you've read, it can be one of your greatest assets. You can build businesses out of competitors' weaknesses. They're also a gold mine of valuable data and can be used to create trust with your prospects and respect in your industry.

So the next time you're wondering how to beat the competition, remember what Michael Corleone said: "Keep your friends close and your enemies closer." It's advice worth keeping in mind.

CHAPTER 14

HOW I HELPED A SaaS BUSINESS GROW OVER 1,000 PERCENT IN UNDER NINE MONTHS

I'M SURE YOU UNDERSTAND THE IMPORTANCE OF GROWTH. It's what turns ideas into businesses and startups into unicorns. But you might not know how to achieve that growth or how to do so quickly. So in this chapter, I'll explain how I helped one promising startup double its revenue in just three months.

JUMPING IN AT THE DEEP END

I joined Spiff, a company that automates sales commission calculations, in early September 2019. I'd met with Jeron Paul, the CEO and founder, and was initially going to be an advisor. The deeper I understood their business, however, the more I wanted to do. This startup was going places, and I wanted to inject a little nitro into their engines.

Helping a company grow is an exhilarating and memorable experience. It's full of ups and downs and forges bonds with people you'll never forget. But as with most entrepreneurs, the call to start another company of my own got the best of me. I've since become a strategic advisor to Spiff and have recruited a talented VP of Sales and Marketing to replace me. As Chief Revenue Officer (CRO), however, I had a blast working with the team.

In my nine months as CRO, we grew the company by over 1,000 percent and successfully secured a $10 million series A investment led by Norwest Venture Partners, EpicVC, and Salesforce Ventures. While I can't share exactly how we did that (otherwise Spiff's competitors might copy it), I can tell you the basics. I'd also like to thank Jeron for his caring leadership and for allowing me to share these details with you now.

So how do you grow a business 1,000 percent in just nine months?

FOCUS ON YOUR CUSTOMERS' SUCCESS OVER EVERYTHING ELSE

Spiff had an amazing product, loyal customers, and a tremendous market opportunity. They just needed some gasoline to add to their fire. My job was to grow revenue, so I dug in, hopped on the phone, and closed the second-largest deal in company history in my first thirty days.

Was it magic? No. We simply focused on making this

customer insanely successful. We created a true hand-in-hand partnership with their 100-plus-person sales team. Startups depend on their customers' success, so by prioritizing that over everything else, we secured top-tier clients.

It's a simple strategy: instead of talking about services or features, you discuss how to make your customers more successful. Listen more than you talk. Understand their pain points, and be authentic about wanting to help. Agree on what success looks like. Sales is a process of listening and helping the other person solve their problem. Use every available resource to help them achieve their goals, and you'll mirror their success.

CLOSE THE CREDIBILITY GAP

Before Spiff, Jeron had already built and sold three businesses. I'd sold two of my own, but Jeron's ability to spot new market opportunities and build solutions for them was like nothing I'd ever seen. I knew Spiff had both an amazing story and the experience to make good on their promises. All I had to do was tell the world.

I successfully pitched to *TechCrunch* and *Forbes*, and re-cruited Aaron Ross, ex-Salesforce Director of Sales and author of *Predictable Revenue*, as an advisor. With this increased credibility from industry influencers, we were able to scale upmarket. We could work with even larger companies and faster, proving that Spiff could resolve their complicated sales commission calculations with ease.

ENSURE THE REVENUE MODEL IS PREDICTABLE AND REPEATABLE

Before you can accelerate growth, you need to understand its causes and how to exploit them. This requires meticulous tracking of sales and marketing metrics. Your team must understand how to improve these metrics, how they impact the growth of the company, and how they affect the team personally and professionally.

Once everyone understands and gets behind growth targets, they're much easier to achieve. People start talking and collaborating. Staff share tips, strategies, and tools. Instead of everyone scrabbling around on their own, the team unifies, and growth skyrockets.

Importantly, you should always document your sales process. Outline the behavior you expect from your sales team, as well as tried-and-tested methods from your best reps. This will make it much easier to train new staff, and more importantly, will ensure you deliver a consistently amazing customer experience to every prospect.

STRENGTHEN THE FINANCIAL MODEL

Once you identify your growth levers, you need to know how much it costs to pull them. Customer acquisition costs (CAC), lifetime value per customer (LTV), visitor-to-lead ratio, lead-to-MQL/SQL ratio, MQL/SQL-to-demo ratio, demo-to-close rate (DTCR), ideal customer profiles (ICP), and more will vary across different sales channels (for definitions of these items, check out the glossary at the end of the book). You need to figure out where your most qualified leads come from so you know where to invest your time and money.

It might be social media, outbound sales, content marketing, paid advertising campaigns, brand strategy, or a number of other growth channels. Find the most cost-effective channel quickly, and then focus your time and resources there rather than attack the market from fifty different angles. It's best to dominate one channel than to be just okay in all of them.

It's all about understanding where you get the most out of each minute and dollar. Yes, I said minute because in the early days your time is just as scarce if not scarcer than your financial resources. Plus, it makes focus clear. Always strive to do less, better.

TALK TO YOUR CUSTOMERS

All growth starts with understanding the people who are buying from you. As soon as I joined Spiff, I started talking with their customers, reading their reviews, and understanding their strengths and weaknesses, who loved the product and why, where they needed to improve, and how Spiff compared to competitors.

There is so much to learn from customers. You don't need to speak to all of them—just a handful will do. Find their similarities, where they hang out, what they do, and why they chose your business over others. Then you can double down in these areas for some fast and easy wins.

But most importantly, make sure you're always checking in with customers to ensure they're happy. Your existing customers are your most valuable asset, so deliver on your brand promise and keep them thrilled with your service so they recommend it to friends.

KNOW YOUR COMPETITION AND MARKET POSITION

Also, check out your competition. I made it clear that Spiff had to take the high road and never bash their competitors. In fact, they were to do the opposite and recommend that prospects research competitors to build trust and show confidence. While you might lose a few deals, you'll quickly learn why and can use that insight to improve.

But whatever you do, don't belittle your competitors. Don't send your prospects a list of trick questions to ask the competition or a spreadsheet with false or inflated statements comparing you and them. This happened to me while researching the market (I won't say who did this), and it was very disappointing to see. Just focus on your customers' success, and you'll win more often than not.

Business is a team sport. I say this all the time because it's true. You need to unlock your team's strengths to create one incredible, defensible growth strategy. This is how you grow a company 100 percent in ninety days. It's never done by one person alone. The better the team, the faster you'll grow. The best investment you can make is in your team. Respect that, and you'll go far.

RESOURCES ON ACQUISITIONS

CHAPTER 15

KNOW YOUR EXITS

When Your Startup Is
Most Likely to Be Acquired

WHILE SELLING IS EVERY FOUNDER'S DREAM, the acquisition process can be a nightmare. It's long, tedious, and bureaucratic. It can even pull you away from running your business. And in the long run, no acquisition is guaranteed.

Despite the drawbacks, you're sixteen times more likely to be bought than reaching an IPO.[11] So to achieve your lifelong dream of a sale, you need to play the odds in your favor. In other words, you need to know *when* to sell.

There are several important data points that can help you plan your exit. Understand these, and you'll not only know *when* to

---

11 Jason Rowley, "Here's How Likely Your Startup Is to Get Acquired at Any
   Stage," *TechCrunch*, May 17, 2017, https://techcrunch.com/2017/05/17/
   heres-how-likely-your-startup-is-to-get-acquired-at-any-stage.

sell but *how* to go about the sales process. Let's explore them now.

WHAT MOTIVATES BUYERS?

To understand when to sell, you need to know what motivates buyers. Putting yourself in their shoes can shed light on their strategy, and ultimately, give you an edge in negotiations. So let's first establish what buyers' goals are.

Typically, acquisitions happen for two reasons:

1. **Strategic:** A strategic acquisition aims to increase the buyer's revenue or help them enter an emerging market quickly. A larger company will see strategic value in absorbing a startup when its technologies, teams, customers, or all of the above prove valuable. When Verizon acquired AOL, for example, it was interested in AOL's mobile advertising technology and how it would help grow its revenue and better serve customers.

2. **Financial:** Financial buyers are often private equity (PE) firms with the capital and strategies to grow a company and raise its value. Their ultimate goal is to build it to an IPO, sell its share, or sell the company at a higher value in the future. In 2017, for example, Great Hill Partners bought ZoomInfo for $200 million and then resold it a year later for $400 million to its main competitor, DiscoverOrg. Typically, a PE firm will replace the management team, accelerate growth, and then look to sell the company again.

Now that you know what motivates buyers, let's take a look at what makes a startup an attractive prospect.

WHAT ARE BUYERS LOOKING FOR?

Buyers tend to look for three things:

1. NOVELTY

Hundreds of thousands of startups are created and sold every year. Buyers are spoiled for choice, so to stand a chance of being acquired, yours needs to stand out due to your ARR, technology, or overall proposition. You don't have to be unique, but you do have to be compelling.

2. SIZE

Most financial private equity buyers won't show interest until a startup has $10 million annual recurring revenue (ARR). Even an interested strategic acquirer may not show interest until the $5 million ARR threshold. Smaller startups are less attractive to buyers because there is less to financially or strategically gain through acquisition. These startups usually fall under a buyer's "wait and see" category.

Size matters because it's a strong indication of:

- A healthy and growing customer base.
- Market experience and success.

- Proof of the startup's concept and model work.
- A higher chance of success in reaching an IPO.

3. MARKET VISIBILITY

Small yet immensely profitable startups can struggle to find interested buyers because so much attention and opportunity is paid to the larger startups. To counter this, ensure your startup's story is strong enough to get people talking about it.

Since size often correlates with fundraising stages and fundraising stages influence how easy (or not) it is to sell your startup, let's take a look at your chances of acquisition at each stage of fundraising.

THE BEST TIME TO SELL

In an article for *TechCrunch*,[12] Jason Rowley brilliantly elucidates the correlation between the funding stage and the probability of acquisition. Rather than repeat his experiment with my own data, I'll draw some conclusions from a very telling graph within the article and present them here.

Every round of funding is called a series. The first is series A, then series B, and so on. The graph indicates that most startups are acquired during series E. But that's not the same as saying you're most likely to be acquired at that stage. First, few startups ever make it to that round—most have either been

---

12 Jason Rowley, "Here's How Likely Your Startup Is to Get Acquired at Any Stage."

acquired or IPO'd. Those that do, such as the $1.8 billion raised by the unicorn Carta,[13] are usually financing a vision that's grown much larger in scope.

Cumulative Proportion of Acquired Companies by Stage

Based on Funding Data from US Tech Companies Founded between 2003 and 2013

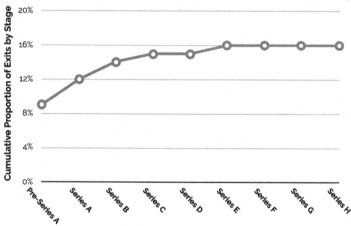

Graph taken from TechCrunch.

So when is the best time to be acquired?

Well, there's not much difference between stages C, D, and E. The cumulative number of startups acquired at these stages plateaus at around 15 to 16 percent. The biggest jumps occur between:

---

13 Connie Loizos, "Carta Was Just Valued at $1.7 Billion by Andreessen Horowitz, in a Deal Some See as Rich," *TechCrunch*, May 6, 2019, https://techcrunch.com/2019/05/06/carta-was-just-valued-at-1-7-billion-by-andreessen-horowitz-in-a-deal-some-see-as-rich.

- Pre-series A and series A: around 4 percent.
- Series A and series B: around 2 percent.
- Series B and series C: around 1 percent.

Based on this data, you're more likely to be acquired at series C than series B, series B than series A, and even more strikingly, series A than pre-series A. This is because the more you demonstrate your attractiveness to investors, the greater their interest in you.

These results probably won't surprise you. Successful funding rounds are typically regarded as proof you have something special to offer. But while it can be tempting to draw lessons from this simple analysis, the chances of you being acquired come down to your *expectations* as much as anything else.

Let me explain.

The graph indicates you're more likely to be acquired further down the fundraising route. However, there is a distinction between the *proportion* of companies that exit at each stage and when you *should* exit. This is a personal choice, to an extent, since you might want to hold on to raise more funding and command a higher purchase price later.

Bear in mind, though, you need to put in some serious grind to progress from one stage to the next, with no guaranteed outcomes. And on top of fundraising, you still have a business to run and grow. It's easy to focus too much on raising funding and not enough on your business. While the effect of this might be small initially, it can quickly disrupt an otherwise healthy, profitable business.

A better strategy, one that considers the survival rates of early-stage startups as well as the chances of being acquired or ever reaching an IPO, might be to quit chasing big numbers and accept an offer when it's on the table.

While it's true that only 8 to 9 percent of startups in this data set ever got acquired at pre-series A, *60 percent don't ever make it to the next stage.* So why not get out when the going is good? You can then focus on new projects, goals, and ambitions, applying what you've learned to advance your entrepreneurial career.

So to recap, then:

1. Most startups are acquired at series E, but few make it that far.

2. You're more likely to be acquired the more funding you raise. However, fundraising is tougher in the early stages and can pull focus from running your business. In other words, it's a risky strategy if an exit is your goal.

3. An offer at pre-series A is uncommon yet *highly desirable.* If it's on the table at that stage, statistically, you should take it.

CHAPTER 16

HOW TO ESTIMATE THE VALUE OF YOUR SaaS STARTUP

IF YOU'RE GOING TO SELL YOUR SAAS STARTUP, you'll need a professional valuation. Your buyer will insist on it at some stage during the acquisition process. But before this happens, you need a reference point to grab buyers' attention. It doesn't need to be accurate, but it should be an evidence-based guess that gets your foot in the door and keeps it there.

Nothing riles investors more than overvaluation, but you don't want to undersell yourself either. Do your homework, and the numbers will speak for themselves. Estimate the value of your startup correctly, and you'll not only attract more buyers, but you'll be in a strong position come negotiation time.

DEVISING THE RIGHT METHODOLOGY

Every startup is different, so you need to choose the methodology that best fits your business. It's all about measuring performance now, which is easy, and in the future, which involves uncertainty.

All valuations start with applying a multiple to current earnings or revenue:

Estimated value = (earnings or revenue) × multiple

So let's explore each of these variables in turn.

EARNINGS
Seller Discretionary Earnings (SDE)

If you own and run a small business, apply the multiple to SDE. This is your profit after deducting operating expenses and cost of goods from revenue and then adding your compensation back in.

Why add in your compensation? If you're taking the lion's share of responsibility, you're taking the lion's share of the profits as compensation and enjoying the capital and tax advantages of being a small business owner. Adding owner compensation into SDE, therefore, gives a truer measure of earnings potential.

Here's the formula to calculate your SDE:

SDE = (Revenue – Operating Expenses – Cost of Goods) + Your Compensation

Earnings Before Interest, Taxes, Depreciation and Amortization (EBITDA)

Once you're big enough to employ a management team, things start getting trickier. You can't add your compensation into earnings, as you're no longer the only one running the show. This becomes a real cost and must be left out of the earnings calculation along with your other expenses. Instead, apply the multiple to EBITDA.

EBITDA can be calculated in two ways,[14] and as long as you're consistent (not switching back and forth to get the highest number), you can choose whichever results in a truer representation of your startup's earning potential:

1. EBITDA = Operating Profit + Depreciation and Amortization

2. EBITDA = Net Profit + Interest + Taxes + Depreciation and Amortization

WHEN TO USE REVENUE

If your EBITDA or SDE is zero because you're investing heavily in growth, consider applying the multiple to revenue. It's pretty common for SaaS businesses to accept short-term losses in

---

14 Claire Boyte-White, "The Formula for Calculating EBITDA (With Examples)," *Investopedia*, April 19, 2021, https://www.investopedia.com/ask/answers/031815/what-formula-calculating-ebitda.asp.

return for growth.[15] You might focus on product development and marketing right now but pull back on these expenses when you scale.

But before choosing revenue, remember you need to prove you're capable of such growth. Fail to do so, and your valuation collapses. Reinforce it with projections, market research, and other evidence to back up your number.

DECIDING THE MULTIPLE

You can derive SDE, EBITDA, and revenue from a balance sheet in minutes. The multiple, however, is a lot more complicated. Where earnings is a verifiable number, the multiple takes into account myriad business, market, and performance factors.

I could write a book on these, so I won't go into them now. Instead, I'll focus on the key things you need to determine where your startup fits within a multiple range.

Between Q4 2014 and Q4 2018, Crunchbase reported a median multiple ranging from 4.43 to 9.32, with an average of 6.69.[16] This was for public SaaS companies only, but it's a good place to start. Now you need to establish where you fit along this spectrum. To justify a higher multiple, your startup should:

---

15 George Deeb, "Growth vs. Profit: What should rising startups focus on first?" *TheNextWeb*, March 16, 2014, https://thenextweb.com/news/growth-vs-profit-startups-focus-first.

16 Sammy Abdullah, "SaaS Valuations are Unshakeable," *CrunchBase*, November 26, 2018, https://about.crunchbase.com/blog/saas-valuations.

- Run by itself or with very little involvement from you.
- Have been operating successfully for over a year (the longer the better).
- Demonstrate growth potential.

You might be able to tick points one and two now. To tick the third, you'll need to review some success metrics, including the following.

CHURN

Churn measures lost income through net customer losses or downsized commitments. For example, if you have 1,000 customers at the start of the month and only 900 at the end, including any new ones you acquired, your churn rate would be 10 percent. Or if your customer numbers were steady but 100 downgraded their subscriptions, your churn rate (for that subscription tier) would also be 10 percent.

Churn is an effective measure of customer loyalty and the quality of the product or service on offer, but for it to be meaningful, you should compare your churn rate with that of the industry to assess if yours is better. The better your churn rate (ideally it'll be negative), the more upward pressure on the multiple.

CUSTOMER ACQUISITION COST (CAC)

Overspending on customer acquisition impacts the value of your business, so you want to keep the CAC low. Burning cash to win new customers is a short-lived strategy that often leads to startups failing. Investors don't want to throw good money after bad, so you'll need to demonstrate a reason for a high CAC if you want to keep that multiple high.

LIFETIME VALUE OF CUSTOMER (LTV)

A high LTV might justify a higher CAC or other revenue losses and is a useful way to target customers who offer the best returns. For example, you might pay a higher cost to acquire customers that regularly upgrade or purchase other products and services, as their lifetime value is so much higher.

When deciding what multiple to apply to your earnings or revenue, consider churn, CAC, and LTV in tandem for deeper insight. Each plays an important role. But combined, they offer a more complete view of your business's growth potential.

Once you've reviewed these metrics, you'll have a good idea of where the needle falls on that multiple range.

BRINGING IT ALL TOGETHER

Let's review what you've read in this chapter. To correctly estimate the value of your startup, you need to do the following:

1. **Decide which methodology is most appropriate:** SDE, EBITDA, or revenue. If you own and run a small business, SDE will suit you in 99 percent of cases. Choose EBITDA

if you're larger and share operational responsibilities with others or revenue if you're projecting massive growth.

2. **Determine an evidence-based multiple:** Use CrunchBase or other startup reports to establish a range of multiples for similar businesses to your own. Then decide where your startup fits using success metrics like churn, CAC, and LTV (reviewed in tandem) alongside age and operational demand.

3. **Apply the multiple to your earnings or revenue:** This gives you an approximate value with which you can start conversations with buyers. Explain how you derived the multiple so buyers trust the figure. They might challenge your methodology, but since you've done your homework, you'll be able to defend it.

The more data you have, the better your valuations can be. Don't gloss over things that might impact the health of your business, and you'll have confidence in the final figure. You might even find the professional opinion matches yours.

CHAPTER 17

HOW TO PREPARE YOUR STARTUP FOR ACQUISITION IN JUST SIX STEPS

FINALLY, SOMEONE HAS OFFERED TO BUY YOUR STARTUP.

You've been waiting years for this moment. You feel euphoric, excited. Dreams of life post-acquisition flash through your mind.

But then the nerves kick in.

How on earth will you prepare for this acquisition?

The hard work isn't quite over yet. If you fail to prepare, or do so poorly, you could deter the buyer, hurt your valuation, and net yourself less money.

Then there's your team. Are they aligned with this new company? What can you do to make the transition easier for them?

I've been through the acquisition process several times, with two successful exits under my belt. So I'd like to share what I've learned. Hopefully, it'll give you a smooth ride to the finish line.

STEP 1: DON'T STOP GROWING

Acquisition offers are just that: offers. They're not set in stone until the very last moment. So yes, be excited. Yes, prepare well. But whatever happens, don't neglect the growth of your business. Stay the course. Keep to your targets. After all, it'll only improve your company's value, and you won't risk your startup stalling if the deal falls through.

STEP 2: DO YOUR HOMEWORK

Acquisition stories are everywhere, good and bad, so learn from them. Avoid others' mistakes. Find out how the acquisition will affect you and your teams. Reach out to other entrepreneurs, particularly those in your industry, who've sold businesses before. They'll have practical advice to navigate the process successfully.

STEP 3: GET YOUR RECORDS IN ORDER

The buyer is going to audit the hell out of you, so consult your accounting, legal, and HR departments, and get your house in order, including all relevant paperwork. Discrepancies during due diligence can kill acquisitions, or at minimum, hurt your valuation. So if recordkeeping is your Achilles' heel, get it fixed *fast*—your buyer will be looking for mistakes.

STEP 4: HIRE PROFESSIONALS

Enlist some outside help for due diligence. While I'm sure your staff is competent, we've already established in step 3 that mistakes can kill a sale. So hiring professionals with specialized knowledge of acquisitions and the necessary preparations can be a big help. Here are some to consider.

CPA Firm: A pre-sale financial audit gives the buyer independent legal confirmation of the veracity of your records. This helps grease the wheels, so to speak, and will inspire confidence and trust.

Valuation Firm: Unsurprisingly, the buyer wants to pay as little as possible. Get your business independently valued, and you've got an accurate, fair number that will hold water under intense buyer scrutiny.

Financial/Accounting Services: Expect to prepare pro forma statements, financial schedules, expense accounts, revenue reports, and much more. The buyer may also ask for earnings predictions and forecasts to gain an understanding of cash flow, or even multiyear projections. Don't overwhelm your accounting staff—that leads to mistakes. Get some outside help.

Law Firm: A great firm will help your staff organize and standardize legal documents that the buyer requests. It might also alleviate the stress of communicating with the buyer's own legal counsel.

While hiring outside support will cost you, their specialist skillsets leave little to chance. With a crack team of professionals behind you, you'll all but guarantee a successful acquisition.

STEP 5: COMMUNICATE YOUR EXPECTATIONS

You and the buyer have different goals. Therefore, it's important to weigh your expectations against those of the buyer to avoid trouble. It's not just about the money—think about your life *after* the acquisition ends.

For example, you should be able to answer these questions:

- Are you staying on, and if so, what role and responsibilities will you have?
- Will you have any say in decisions?
- How will your product mesh with the buyer's offerings and strategies?
- Is this how you see your product being used?

If your expectations don't align with those of the buyer, you're jeopardizing your long-term happiness. Some founders regret selling for this very reason.

STEP 6: LOOK FOR A CULTURE FIT

I'm sure you want the very best for your business and your employees, but it's easy to be suckered in by a great offer and neglect establishing whether or not the buyer is the right fit. Misaligned cultures cause painful transitions, so you need to understand the buyer's values and beliefs and how their mission statement supports these. Are these ideas that you and your team can stand behind?

Being acquired is a bit like selling a house. You want

the best price and assurance the new owners will take good care of it. To do that, you need to keep it clean, fix anything that's broken or missing, and contract specialists to obtain independent valuations. You also need to vet your buyer to ensure a smooth transition for everyone involved. Follow the six steps above, and you'll walk away with more money, fewer headaches, and unassailable confidence you did the right thing.

CHAPTER 18

WHAT TO EXPECT FROM THE SIX LEGAL STAGES OF AN ACQUISITION

NOTHING DERAILS AN ACQUISITION FASTER THAN LEGAL. It's the most critical aspect of a sale, but often it's ugliest. Fail to understand the legal process of selling your company, and you might end up with a lower purchase price, or worse, no sale at all.

Legal is dry, but it's not hard. You can think of it as a six-stage journey. The further you progress, the more serious your buyer, and the likelier you'll close the sale. I've listed these stages below. Study them well and you'll find acquisitions needn't be so intimidating.

(Please note: I've listed these stages in chronological order, but the steps might intermingle a little.)

STAGE 1: THE LETTER OF INTENT (LOI)

An LOI is the first sign of serious buyer interest. It's a rough draft of how the sale will go down, but with plenty of negotiation room. You or the buyer can write the LOI, but both of you must sign it. An LOI typically includes:

- Purchase price
- Due diligence requirements
- Applicable deposit
- Exclusivity period
- Any other relevant terms and conditions

While an LOI is nonbinding, it commits you to a period of exclusivity (in return for a deposit) while the buyer pops the hood of your business and takes a look inside. The LOI should, therefore, include a nondisclosure agreement (NDA) to protect your data, intellectual property, and other sensitive company information.

STAGE 2: DUE DILIGENCE

Due diligence is an audit on steroids. The buyer will analyze your financial metrics and projections, technology, staff, liens, debts, creditors, and lots more with the precision of a forensic pathologist. It can be a stressful time, but remember the buyer is ensuring there are no nasty surprises after the deal closes.

My best advice to you here (unless you're selling a very small business) is to lawyer up. Hire the best mergers and acquisitions lawyer you can find, and follow their lead. While you can do most due diligence on your own, you'll need expert advice to speed up the process and avoid mistakes that may cost you time, or worse, the sale itself.[17]

STAGE 3: THE PURCHASE AGREEMENT

The purchase agreement is a legally binding document that cements the outcome of negotiations and commits you and the buyer to the sale. Again, either of you can write the purchase agreement, but don't sign it until your lawyer has looked over the details and assured you it's safe to do so.

Pay particular attention to any guarantees or obligations on your side. For example, the buyer might've asked you to resolve an issue that arose during due diligence within a certain time frame. While this is normal, you don't want to be on the hook for something years after the sale. Your post-sale responsibilities and liabilities should be few[18] and expire after no longer than a year (ideally).

Your lawyer really earns their bread here. Hire someone good who has your interests at heart. You need an expert, so don't "bootstrap" this part of the acquisition process. Purchase

17 Joe Mont, "How M&A Due Diligence Goes Wrong," *Compliance Week*, January 27, 2015, https://www.complianceweek.com/how-manda-due-diligence-goes-wrong/3404.article.

18 Jessica Benford Powell, "Seller Beware? 4 Key Features of Business Sale Transactions that Sellers Should be Familiar with Before Negotiating," *Ryley Carlock & Applewhite*, March 14, 2019, https://www.rcalaw.com/seller-beware-4-key-features-of-business-sale-transactions-that-sellers-should-be-familiar-with-before-negotiating.

agreements can stretch to hundreds of pages of dense legalese. It's anything but light reading.

STAGE 4: BUYER PAYMENT TERMS

Ideally, you want a cash sale. On the buyer side, however, this won't always be possible. The buyer might need financing from the bank. In this case, the sale hinges upon a credit decision, and you should get assurances before signing the purchase agreement.

Some buyers might also ask for seller financing where you let them pay in installments after a down payment. Obviously, this is riskier than a cash deal. If the buyer defaults, you have to go through the courts to settle up, and who knows what could happen to your business in the meantime.

That said, if your lawyer thinks it's okay, a seller financing deal beats no deal if you're in a hurry to sell. Either way, it's crucial you agree to buyer payment terms in advance of signing the purchase agreement.

STAGE 5: LOCAL LAWS

Be mindful of how local laws affect the sale. There will be certain rules to follow before, during, and after the sale for you and the buyer. Be sure to follow them, or local regulators might delay or halt your sale. You might even face financial penalties. Some things to consider:

- **Liens (debt obligations using your property as collateral) and other debts.** If you can't settle what's owed to creditors, inform the buyer of what's outstanding. Contact your creditors, too, to ensure they'll offer the same line of credit to the buyer; otherwise, you might have to settle before the exchange of ownership takes place.
- **Shareholders.** If you don't have any, great. Otherwise, you might need their approval before selling the business, as well as offering them the chance to sell their shares in advance of the acquisition.
- **Taxes.** Sales tax, for example, varies from state to state. In some states, you're responsible for *paying* sales tax, but in others, you're responsible for *collecting* sales tax from customers. In either case, ensure nothing is outstanding before exchanging ownership.

STAGE 6: TRANSFER OF OWNERSHIP

Phew. You're almost there. Once you've parried and countered your way through negotiations, purchase agreements, and state law, the final step is to legally hand over your business to the new owner. There's very little that can go wrong at this stage. All that's left is a wedge of contracts to sign, and that's it. You're home free.

I'd just like to state for the sake of clarity that I'm not a lawyer, and in no way should you consider the tips above as legal advice. I've simply outlined the legal framework I've observed in many acquisitions, including my own. At the very least, this will prepare you for discussions with your lawyer and can make preparations a little easier for both of you.

CHAPTER 19

DUE DILIGENCE
AND HOW TO SURVIVE IT

NOTHING QUITE TAKES THE SHINE OFF AN ACQUISITION like due diligence.

It's long, tedious, and often stressful.

After the elation of the offer, it's like a bucket of cold water over your head.

Well, as someone who's been acquired twice, I can quite confidently say that yes, due diligence is a pain, but there is a right and a wrong way to go about it.

I'm going to explain the right way.

But first...

WHAT IS DILIGENCE?

Diligence is convincing the buyer your startup is as good as you say it is. Like buying a used car, they'll kick the tires, take a test drive, ask many questions, and sometimes find ways to haggle down the value. So if your treads are worn smooth and your odometer is busted, you'll put the sale—or your asking price—at risk.

The buyer's mission during this stage of the acquisition is to find the skeletons in your closet. They're looking for troublesome contracts, liabilities, ongoing litigations, intellectual property disputes, or account discrepancies. Due diligence will, therefore, affect every one of your departments, particularly legal, accounting, and HR.

ACCOUNTING, FINANCIAL, AND TAX DILIGENCE

This is where you'll spend most of your time. It's also the principal area of due diligence a buyer will leverage to lower your startup's valuation. Don't let them! Consider and prepare for the following.

BUSINESS PERFORMANCE AND HEALTH

- Do you have annual and quarterly records for the last three to five years that showcase the performance and health of your startup's finances?
- Do projections for this year fall below or above your startup's budget?

- Should a quality of earnings report be conducted?
- What is the status and health of your startup's assets and liens?
- What does your company's EBITDA suggest about the performance and health of the startup?

FUTURE GROWTH

- Are profits increasing or decreasing? By how much?
- What are the financial forecasts for the coming years, and how accurate are they?
- Do you have enough money and assets to continue operating comfortably, particularly from the period of diligence to the projected close date of the deal?
- How much working capital do you need to continue growing and operating the business, and how is working capital defined?

TAXES

- Do you have tax returns and other related documents for the past three to five years?
- Are there any local, state, foreign, or federal tax regulations the buyer should know about?
- What are the tax implications of the acquisition deal itself?

ACCURACY AND TRANSPARENCY

- Have all your financial and accounting records been properly checked for errors and discrepancies?
- Are there any outstanding debts? How and when will those be repaid?
- Have your financial documents, accounts, and statements been audited by a third party? How recently?
- Are all liabilities, current or contingent, laid out in these financial documents?
- Are your future projections reasonable and based on believable trends in your finances?
- Do accounts receivable have any issues that need to be disclosed?
- Have any capital expenditures been deferred? Is this affecting your operating budget?

LEGAL DILIGENCE

If you have legal issues nipping at your feet, expect the buyer to give you a wide berth. It's up to you to convince the buyer that you're squeaky clean, or at the very least, have ongoing issues under control. Legal diligence involves matters such as the following.

CLAIMS AND LITIGATIONS

- Do you have a complete record of all files on all pending litigations, claims, complaints, and so on?

- Are any of the complaints current or ongoing? What about legal claims in arbitration?
- What are the sources of these legal matters? Are any from government sources like the FDA or FTC?

REGULATORY AND ANTITRUST ISSUES

- If your startup is in a regulated industry, is there a governing body with the power to approve or deny the acquisition?
- Has the startup had any regulatory or antitrust issues in the past?
- Are there any consolidation issues that would negatively impact approval?

ENVIRONMENTAL ISSUES

- Are there any ecological liabilities or obligations, whether past or current?
- Do records exist of past environmental audits or reports, particularly for a company's properties and facilities?
- Do you produce or use any hazardous materials, and if so, how are they handled and/or disposed of?

INTELLECTUAL PROPERTY DILIGENCE

Often, buyers are interested in obtaining your technology or intellectual property. So in this area of due diligence, you want to demonstrate that you've adequately protected your IP.

PROPERTIES

- Do you own any patents, including foreign ones or pending applications?
- What about registered, common law trademarks or copyrighted products and materials?
- Do you use any third-party licensed software, machines, or other products, and how essential are they to the business?

SECURITY

- Has your company performed the necessary steps to protect its intellectual property assets?
- How do you preserve confidentiality? Are there any issues with past or current employees infringing on this agreement?
- Have any trade secrets been leaked?

LEGAL

- Are there any ongoing litigations or disputes over patents, intellectual properties, licensing, or other relevant matters?
- Are there any third-party companies infringing on your startup's intellectual property rights?
- What other liens or issues exist with regard to your intellectual properties?

TEAM AND EMPLOYEE DILIGENCE

Likewise, some buyers are interested in your teams. They might like your office locations or your employees' specialties. So be prepared to explain to the buyer how you manage, contract, and compensate your teams.

ORGANIZATIONAL STRUCTURE AND FIT

- What's your startup structure, and what background can you provide on its employees?
- Which employees are essential, and will they stay on after the acquisition?
- How quickly will your employees integrate into the buyer's structure?
- What are your company policies, and how do these align with those of the buyer?

COMPENSATION AND INCENTIVES

- Can you provide a summary of compensation and employee benefits, including pensions, deferred compensation, retirement plans, and non-cash benefits (company cars and so on)?
- How much will the acquisition cost in terms of severance and other layoff benefits?
- Will key personnel need an incentive to stay?

OTHER ISSUES
- Have there been any labor disputes in the past or currently?
- What about internal issues between employees or management?

SALES AND MARKETING DILIGENCE

The buyer might also be interested in absorbing your market share. They'll certainly be curious about your customers because they will be acquiring them in the deal too.

CUSTOMERS
- Who are your target customers and audiences?
- How loyal are customers, and how satisfied are they with your product or service?
- Are these customers expected to persist after the acquisition?

SALES AND REVENUE
- Are sales/revenue affected by seasonality?
- How much revenue is generated by the top customers?
- How do you incentivize sales staff (if at all)?

MARKETING

- Is marketing handled in-house or through an agency?
- Are there detailed records of the market your startup serves?
- How do your marketing messages align with the buyers?
- How will the acquisition affect your competitiveness in the market?

Feeling a little overwhelmed? I get it. Due diligence is that 500-pound gorilla standing in the way of the finish line. But if you prepare well, answer these questions, and provide the right evidence to support your answers, diligence should be a breeze. And remember you don't have to do it alone—hire some expert assistance, and you'll be over that line with a check in your pocket in no time.

CHAPTER 20

HOW TO NEGOTIATE A LETTER OF INTENT (LOI) THAT CLOSES AN ACQUISITION DEAL ON YOUR TERMS

PICTURE THIS FOR A MOMENT:

A buyer is interested in your startup.

You've spent days chatting back and forth via email.

You might even have met in person.

Now your buyer is ready to send you a letter of intent (LOI) to buy your business.

This is a moment you've spent the last five-plus years working toward, and you can finally see the finish line.

Your smartphone vibrates. An email from the buyer has landed in your inbox.

You open the email, which is courteous and enthusiastic, and the attached draft of the LOI.

Wait a minute, you think. Your smile fades. The terms of the LOI aren't what you expected, with most items skewed in the buyer's favor.

This a typical example of what can go wrong during an LOI negotiation.

The LOI is the first sign of serious interest, but it's also an invitation to the negotiation table. Deferring tough conversations might speed up acquisition, but failing to negotiate early puts you at a disadvantage.

And believe me, *everything* on an LOI is negotiable, regardless of what the buyer might argue.

When you enter the exclusivity period, power shifts from you to the buyer. It's therefore crucial you negotiate everything in advance and have a solid legal framework so you can proceed with the sale with confidence.

To help, here are a few things to consider.

GET YOUR HOUSE IN ORDER

Finish as much pre-sale due diligence as possible. A little hard work now pays dividends further along in the acquisition process, leaving fewer surprises or kinks to iron out later. Yes, it might take longer to close the deal, but if your buyer is talking LOI, you know they're serious, and it makes sense to get your house in order to make the sale go through smoothly.

LAWYER UP

Preparation is a powerful ally in the acquisition process. You won't be the buyer's first acquisition, nor will you be their last, so don't underestimate them. They'll test you for weaknesses, and unless you happen to be well versed in M&A law, it'll be legal. Buyers will have M&A lawyers or even whole teams working to secure the best outcome for them.

Hire counsel to escort you through these legally choppy waters. Not every buyer will use the law to exploit you, but there will be elements of the negotiation (the definition of company debt, for example) that are open to interpretation, and they'll push *their* interpretation over yours.

NEGOTIATE A TIMELINE AND EXCLUSIVITY PERIOD

Deadlines manage the buyer's and your expectations, but you don't have to set your time by the buyer's watch.

For example, your buyer might want due diligence done quickly but also a long exclusivity period so they can scrutinize your business without the pressure of competing offers. They might even bulldoze through negotiations to pressure you into accepting terms in their favor.

Set an appropriate timeline that includes an exclusivity period of thirty days or less (seven days if you can get it!).

Provide ample time to complete due diligence and other negotiations.

WHAT'S THE PURCHASE PRICE, AND HOW WILL THEY PAY?

Once you've agreed upon a reasonable number, cash settlement is better for you and the buyer, unless your buyer is another company. In this case, you might want to swap stock to own equity in this new entity (the buyer may resist this, however).

Whether you want to own stock in this new entity instead of receiving cash depends on a number of factors, such as the historical performance of the buying company, what their post-acquisition plans are, your immediate cash needs (for example, do you need seed money for a new business?), and so on.

For the avoidance of doubt, negotiate a final number *without conditions*, such as financing, conditional pricing, or stock swaps when you have no interest in the new entity. You don't want to waste time on a deal if the buyer can't give you what you want.

If price is a sticking point, consider an earnout to close the gap. Earnouts are agreements where you receive future payments on the condition of certain financial goals being met. A buyer might agree to the purchase price plus a percentage of revenue on future sales for a limited time, for example. Buyers don't usually like earnouts, however, as it creates uncertainty and restricts what they can do with the business.

If you need an earnout, apply it to revenue only. Profit will likely suffer in the short term given the costs to transition to a new owner. To avoid losing out on a factor that is no longer under your control, calculate earnout on something steadier, like revenue.

MINIMIZE EXPOSURE ON REPS AND WARRANTIES

Beware of your buyer weaponizing fundamental representations and warranties. These are legal assertions of facts relating to your business and how you'll respond should those facts turn out to be false. Buyers may selectively choose the representations that require the most stringent warranties, potentially to your disadvantage.

For example, your buyer wants to avoid any nasty surprises such as misrepresentation or fraud. In this case, you'll refund 100 percent of the purchase price. But they also want to protect intellectual property (IP) or other important assets that might affect the value of the business post-sale, and this is a negotiation point.

For SaaS businesses, for example, your IP is everything. It's what your customers pay for: the software, the implementation, the code that powers your product or service. However, competitors' products, cyberthreats, and regulatory or market conditions can thwart even the best IP. To avoid overexposing yourself post-acquisition, limit your reps and warranties to 10 percent or less for a period of no more than twelve months.

Obviously the more robust your IP, the better placed you'll be to negotiate. This is why doing as much due diligence *before* signing the LOI is so important.

DECIDE HOW MUCH YOU'LL LEAVE BEHIND

Most buyers will expect you to leave the business cash-free and debt-free. This affects working capital too. Positive working capital will appeal to the buyer, but a negative figure isn't always a bad thing—for example, if you're funding growth using supplier or customer funds. However, buyers won't ignore consistent negative capital, as this could indicate a deeper problem.

You might, therefore, need to negotiate working capital before the sale completes. Just remember this is a point of negotiation and not always a judgment on the long-term potential of your business.

Think of LOI negotiations as going a few rounds in the ring. You'll take a punch here and there, but if you've prepared and studied your opponent and you can stand your ground under punishment, you'll emerge tougher and ready to close on *your* terms.

CHAPTER 21

WHY SELLER FINANCING COULD SAVE YOUR ACQUISITION DEAL FROM DISASTER

WHEN IT'S TIME TO SELL YOUR BUSINESS, you know it in your gut. You might feel burned out or anxious or long for a fresh start. However the feeling manifests, you must act on it quickly. Things move at warp speed in startup land, so if you want the best acquisition deal, you need to move equally fast.

But not all potential buyers have the capital for an acquisition or the means of raising it. They might be waiting on bank financing or a loan from the Small Business Administration (SBA), or simply for their coffers to fill. So what do you do? Trade a sale now for one in the future when your valuation might not be so secure?

Although a cash sale is usually preferred, seller financing, where the buyer enters into an agreement to pay you in installments, opens the door for those who don't have the funds for a cash purchase. With a bigger buyer pool, you stand a better chance of selling at the right price, at the right time, *and* to the right buyer. So let's take a look at what seller financing means and how it could help you.

WHAT IS SELLER FINANCING?

In some ways, seller financing is just like any financing. Instead of selling your company for a lump sum, you agree to let the buyer spread the payments over a number of years after a down payment. Where seller financing differs from, say, a mortgage loan is that the repayment term is much shorter—typically five to seven years maximum—and instead of handing over money, you hand over your business.

HOW DOES IT WORK?

Your buyer might ask for seller financing, or you can use it as a bargaining chip in negotiations. Either way, hire a lawyer to act as an intermediary to ensure the deal is to your advantage. You're taking all the risk here, so ensure there are safety measures in place to protect you from buyer default.

Seller financing usually works like this:

You and the buyer agree on the terms of financing. This includes the down payment, interest rate, term, collateral, and so on. Usually, the business is the collateral, so if the buyer defaults, you can reclaim the business in its entirety. However, you can ask for additional collateral—especially if their credit rating is poor—in the form of property or other assets.

The buyer makes a down payment. Since the repayment terms are shorter, the buyer must put down at least 25 to 35 percent of the purchase price[19] as a down payment. Then a larger installment payment at the end, called a balloon payment, settles the debt.

The buyer signs and files a promissory note. The promissory note is the legal contract that binds the buyer to the installment repayment plan. Ask them to file this for you so you don't have to do it yourself (like I said, you're taking the risk, so the buyer should be doing most of the administrative legwork).

The buyer makes their regular payments. While the buyer repays, the business is under their control. This is where things can go awry. If they run your business into the ground or don't make as much money as they thought they would, they might be unable to repay. You'll then have to go through the courts to reclaim your business and assets. That said, if you did your homework before agreeing to seller financing, the chances of this happening are low.

The buyer makes the final balloon payment. Hurrah! It's done. The buyer has paid you the purchase price in full. Now

19 Elise Moores, "How to Use Seller Financing to Sell or Buy a Business," *FastCapital360*, last modified February 11, 2021, https://www.fastcapital360.com/blog/seller-financing-business.

you can draw a line through this stage of your entrepreneurial career and focus on the future.

WHY SELLER FINANCING CAN CHANGE YOUR LIFE (FOR THE BETTER)

Ninety-nine percent of an acquisition is finding the right buyer. Believe me, this is no easy task. When I sold my first "big" business, Bizness Apps, I had countless offers. Some I pursued but they fell through; others demanded too much of me or my employees or just weren't the right fit. When you've poured years of blood, sweat, and tears into a business, you don't let it go to just anyone—you want someone who'll do great things with it.

Unfortunately, finding someone who is both well funded *and* the right fit can take months, perhaps years, and in that time your business is exposed to all kinds of threats. Think market changes, consumer changes, technology changes—all of which can hurt your valuation (granted, they might boost it, too, but who wants to take that chance?).

A seller financing deal, however, attracts more buyers since you open acquisition offers to those who can only pay in installments. This boosts your chances of finding the right buyer *and* justifies a higher sale price. There are taxation benefits,[20] too, since seller financing results in paying lower "per year" capital gains tax to the IRS than if it had been an all-cash purchase.

---

20 Luke Arthur, "Tax Breaks for Owner Financing," Chron, accessed July 31, 2021, https://smallbusiness.chron.com/tax-breaks-owner-financing-22159.html.

Perhaps the biggest benefit, however, is how a quick sale helps your career. When you're stuck on a train with no enthusiasm for its destination, life is glum. You might be moving forward, but not in the direction you'd like. But if you can sell quickly, and at the right price, you can switch tracks and take your career anywhere you want. Seller financing, then, rather than being a last resort, could be your key to entrepreneurial freedom and a springboard to better things. So keep it up your sleeve when you're ready to sell.

CHAPTER 22

WHY SᴀᴀS BUSINESSES MAKE GREAT ACQUISITIONS FOR FIRST-TIME FLIPPERS

WHEN BUYING A BUSINESS, IT'S IMPORTANT TO KNOW what you want.

The wrong acquisition can ruin your finances and reputation. So if you're unsure of how to start, I recommend researching different business types and industries to figure out which appeals to you most.

In this chapter, I'll cover why SaaS businesses make great acquisitions, especially for first-time buyers, and the things to look out for before making your first offer.

WHAT IS A SAAS BUSINESS?

SaaS stands for software as a service.

In the past, you'd install business software on your computer or a private server. But now you subscribe to the software and run it in the cloud. Salesforce, Adobe, and Shopify, for example, all use the SaaS model.

SaaS therefore saves the cost of hardware, storage, and licensing fees. You get all upgrades for free, along with around-the-clock maintenance and customer support, and you can access the software from any internet-enabled device.

The recurring revenue model pays for maintenance, hosting, customer operations, sales staff, and, of course, the ongoing development of the software. While it's common to see monthly and yearly subscriptions, pay-as-you-go models exist, too, so it's a flexible model.

Now that you know what SaaS is, let's take a look at why these businesses make great acquisitions.

SaaS IS LUCRATIVE AS HELL

SaaS businesses typically have very low overheads. If you're a developer and can do your own sales and marketing, it's the kind of business you can run from your bedroom or shared office space.

Typically, lean, agile SaaS businesses run at around 70 percent profit. That assumes you're doing most of the work or you've found a way to outsource it cheaply (such as using remote teams). If not, that number will drop significantly as you spend more on expensive engineers and growth marketing.

One thing to remember about SaaS margins is they depend on scale. So when you're looking at acquiring your first, you want to ask questions about customer numbers, growth, MRR, ARR, and churn rate to give you an insight into the health and future potential of the business.

Or you could take a punt if you think the technology has enormous potential in the right hands (yours!). You need the experience to develop it and bring it to market, or you need to have a partner with the expertise to do it for you (though you'll need to sweeten the deal with equity).

SaaS Is One of the Easiest Businesses to Flip

Let's assume you're a software engineer or have partnered with one. Building an MVP and taking it to market is a long, difficult road. You'll make countless mistakes along the way. You'll spend months building and even longer marketing. You'll write and present a hundred different pitches to a hundred different people. And even then, you might not find sufficient traction to grow into a full-fledged business.

Buying an existing SaaS business, however, is a much simpler path to profit. It doesn't even need to be very big. All you need is to find something good that needs a little help. The missing element—be it marketing, brand, sales, product, or customer service—should align with your expertise or that of your team. That way, you bring to the table the one thing the business lacks, a kind of "golden ticket" to growth.

SaaS is an extremely competitive market, but with the right skillset, you can carve out a sizable share. You don't have stock to purchase. You don't have inventory to manage. You don't have a long list of suppliers to negotiate with, nor do you need a physical space to sell your products. But you do need a great SaaS product, the servers to host it, a compelling brand story, and—assuming you're not doing everything yourself—a motivated team.

With all that behind you, you can either continue growing the business or move on to something new. You won't be the only one looking to acquire profitable, lean SaaS businesses. The resale market is huge, and so are the profits, should you catalyze growth. So why not use your skill profile to flip SaaS businesses? It's one of the easiest ways to become a serial entrepreneur.

WHAT TO LOOK FOR BEFORE MAKING AN OFFER

If you like what you've read so far, here are five things to research before making your first offer:

Fit: List your strengths, and find a SaaS business that would benefit from them. Once you've identified what's missing, ensure plugging the gap will make the business grow. There's no point in contributing a stellar sales team if the product lags behind competitors on price or performance.

Growth: Flipping SaaS is often a numbers game. Get ARR, MRR, churn rates, and other financial data to project where the business is going. If growth is stalling, find out why and whether or not you can put it back in gear.

Market: How big is the market? Is there potential for expansion? What are competitors doing? Is there a missing story that, if told, would set sales on fire? Answer these questions, and you're primed for pole position.

Technology: Understand the product and its strengths and weaknesses. If it's broken, fix it. Hire a software engineer if you can't assess it yourself. Figure out what you need to do to maintain and develop the technology and how much it will cost.

Team: SaaS businesses are teeming with talent. Decide who you want (if anyone), and then persuade them to stay. There are clear advantages to using existing teams, as they know the business better than you do. However, you might also want a clean slate—especially if the team is the problem.

The acquisition process can be a fickle one, and the better prepared you are, the less stressful the experience will be, especially if it's your first. But whether you're a serial entrepreneur, an angel investor, or just starting out, SaaS has some of the lowest barriers to entry and can be an easy flip with the right skillset.

CHAPTER 23

CHURN, CODE, AND CUSTOMERS

Three Signs a SaaS Business Is Worth Acquiring

EVERY INVESTMENT INVOLVES RISK, and SaaS acquisitions are no different.

Skip due diligence, and you expose your flanks. You might as well toss a coin and hope for the best.

Do your research, however, and you'll know what to acquire and when. Instead of pouring money down the drain, you'll be planting the seeds of phenomenal growth.

So here are the three main areas to focus on before making an offer. Read them carefully, and next time you're ready to buy, you can cherry-pick from the best in the market.

CHURN (AND OTHER IMPORTANT NUMBERS)

Churn is often measured as a percentage of lost revenue. While this can be the result of a net customer loss, it might also be because customers are downsizing or canceling add-ons and so on. Churn is a useful yardstick for measuring customer loyalty, as well as the quality of the product, so low churn is the first sign a business is worth acquiring.

While all businesses aspire to a negative churn rate (a net increase in customers), size and other factors impact results.[21] For example, it's easier and cheaper for small businesses to switch vendors, so you should expect a higher churn rate for small to medium businesses (SMBs). To assess churn, you need a reference, so compare your prospect with similar-sized businesses in the same segment. Also, consider churn over time. If your prospect beats the competition, you could be on to a winner.

Two other important numbers are lifetime value of customer (LTV) and customer acquisition cost (CAC). LTV indicates the total possible income from one customer, including subscriptions, upselling, cross-selling, and other revenue streams. A high LTV can offset revenue losses as well as identify which buyers to target for the best ROI.

Unless the LTV is particularly high, CAC should always be low. It's easy to overspend on marketing (if Adidas can, you can) with the hope it'll equal growth. A high CAC alongside a low LTV and/or high churn rate should ring alarm bells.

---

21 Jarrod Morris, "What's an Acceptable Churn Rate for SaaS Companies?" Graphly, accessed July 31, 2021, https://graphly.io/whats-an-acceptable-churn-rate-for-saas-companies.

Always review churn, LTV, and CAC together so you can assess underlying problems with the business.

CODE: WHO WROTE IT? WHO OWNS IT? IS IT ANY GOOD?

The next area for review is the software. Unless you're an engineer, you'll probably need to hire one or ask a friend to help out here. Even without being a coder, you should, at the very least, understand how the product works on a high level. A modern, well-organized, and well-designed codebase is easy to spot and is the first indication the development team is strong.

Speaking of the development team, you also need to understand who owns the IP. It might be the existing team, but maybe contractors and other vendors have a stake in it too. While multiple parties owning portions of the IP isn't necessarily bad, it does complicate things a bit. To avoid problems once the business scales and life-changing money is at stake, ensure contracts exist to back up everyone's claims.

CUSTOMERS: THE ULTIMATE LITMUS TEST

The right attitude toward customers can cover a multitude of sins. If the product is little more than an MVP, 24/7 customer support can both reassure and delight customers while they await improvements. For more established businesses, great customer experiences reduce churn and encourage referrals and positive reviews, which in turn reduces the CAC.

But that's not all. Finding out what customers say about the business often reveals problems that aren't listed on a spec or balance sheet. There might be issues even the founders aren't aware of. If there's a backlog of support tickets, for example, or a breakdown in communication, there's a good possibility you'll be buying a business that's on the verge of customer collapse.

To avoid this, read every review and testimonial. Reach out to customers, and try the product yourself. See how customer service reps have handled problems in the past. Find out what people are saying on social media. If all you're reading is good news, or at the very least, positive outcomes to challenging situations, you know your prospect has put customers first.

Overall, whether you're a first-time buyer or a serial entrepreneur, SaaS is ripe for flipping. But if you don't know what to look for or you focus on the wrong things, you could be throwing good money after bad. So take my advice: do your homework on the three areas above, and you can be confident your next acquisition will be a profitable one.

CHAPTER 24

HOW TO FINANCE AN ACQUISITION USING AN SBA LOAN

IF YOU WANT TO BUY ANOTHER BUSINESS, don't let a lack of capital hold you back. You're unlikely to land that killer idea the first time, so serial entrepreneurship is your best chance of success. When you spot a business for sale that would thrive under your leadership but your funds are tied up in your current company, consider an SBA loan to finance the acquisition.

HANG ON—WHAT'S THE SBA?

The SBA is a federal agency that helps small businesses get loans. They don't issue loans themselves but instead work with lenders to overcome obstacles to business lending, such as guaranteeing loans, reducing risk, and sourcing capital. On a deeper level, the SBA funds, licenses, and regulates investment funds that lend to small businesses.

Since the SBA helps foster competition and diversity in the US economy, getting an SBA loan to finance an acquisition is relatively simple. Importantly, it doesn't matter whether you've been declined credit before or have a poor credit history—you might still qualify for a loan with the SBA. That said, they do have certain eligibility requirements, including:

- Your business must trade in the US.
- You must have invested in the business yourself.
- You must be a for-profit business.
- You must have tried but been unable to source funding from traditional lenders.

WHY FINANCE AN ACQUISITION WITH THE SBA?

BETTER RATES

When you've run out of other options, the SBA can save a potential acquisition deal. But that's not all. SBA loans are also competitively priced (under 8 percent).[22] As a federal agency, the SBA enforces responsible lending and risk management, so lenders can afford to charge lower rates and fees. You're arguably less exposed to predatory practices when you borrow from the SBA than from subprime business lenders.

---

22 "SBA Loan Rates 2021," *NerdWallet*, April 28, 2021, https://www.nerdwallet.com/article/small-business/sba-loan-rates.

Terms vary from seven to twenty-five years, giving ample time to repay at an affordable monthly premium.

BETTER TERMS

Since the SBA guarantees up to 85 percent of the loan, there's less pressure on you and your current business to shoulder all the risk. You'll rarely pay more than a 10 percent down payment, and if you're borrowing less than $350,000, you won't always need collateral. That said, you will need to sign a personal guarantee to repay the loan in full.

HELP AND SUPPORT

The SBA can be a helpful sidekick during the acquisition process too. You might hit a wall of due diligence and legal wrangling that can deter even the staunchest of entrepreneurs from moving forward. The SBA has a vested interest in your success here and can support you with counseling and learning resources right until you sign the purchase agreement.

HOW TO GET AN SBA LOAN TO FINANCE AN ACQUISITION

The general-use 7(a) loan is the SBA's most popular and is ideal as acquisition finance. You can borrow up to $5 million, which is more than enough for acquisitions of small or even medium-sized businesses. You can only borrow what you can afford to repay, however, and an SBA-approved lender will determine this amount when you apply.

To begin applying for an SBA loan, you first need a list of SBA-approved lenders in your area. Head to the SBA website and fill in some basic details, and their matching tool will produce a list of suitable lenders. Remember, this isn't an application, and those on the list won't necessarily give you a loan. The next step is to apply. The specifics will vary from lender to lender. But be prepared to hand over or have scrutinized the following information:

- **The amount of money** you want to borrow and its purpose.
- **A business plan.** Because you're acquiring a new business, this should include post-acquisition plans and why it's the right acquisition for you.
- **Your financials.** They want evidence you're capable of repaying the loan. Expect to hand over tax filings, balance sheets, P&L statements, and more.
- **Your experience.** They'll want to see your industry expertise in both your current business and the one you're about to buy, should it be in a different sector.
- **Your credit history.** Again, don't stress if your record has a few hiccups. The SBA underwrites a portion of loans and therefore can accept some poor credit applications.
- **Collateral.** How will you collateralize the loan? Will it be stock, property, or other assets? Depending on the lender, you might be able to choose what's on and off the table collateral-wise.

The SBA and the lender will assess your application and return with a decision.

SOME THINGS TO REMEMBER

PLAN EARLY BECAUSE GETTING AN SBA LOAN TAKES TIME

If you've already found a business you like, apply for the SBA loan now. As you might know, dealing with federal agencies is a long and bureaucratic process. You could wait a few weeks before receiving a decision and perhaps a week or two longer to receive funds. Get the ball rolling as soon as possible so you don't lose out to another buyer.

7(A) INTEREST RATES ARE VARIABLE

The 7(a) SBA loan type is calculated on a variable base rate (a rate pegged to another, such as the LIBOR rate, for example) plus a markup negotiated with your lender. When this base rate changes, the rate on your loan changes, so be prepared to pay a bit more or less each month over the term of the loan.

NEGOTIATE, NEGOTIATE, NEGOTIATE

You need to negotiate fees, repayments, collateral, interest, and so on with the lender. The SBA limits what the lender can charge, but rest assured the lender will seek the best out-come for themselves. Don't be afraid to negotiate the terms, especially if you're in a position of strength, such as having a good credit rating.

SBA loans are one of the best forms of credit available. The interest rates are low, and the repayment terms fair. If you already own a business and are eyeing up another, don't fret if you don't have the capital to finance the acquisition. The SBA can help you seal the deal.

CHAPTER 25

GLOSSARY OF TECHNICAL TERMS, ACRONYMS, AND METRICS

I HATE JARGON, AND I'M SURE YOU DO TOO. Unfortunately, entrepreneurship is racked with terms and acronyms that make your head spin. Where possible, I defined these as they arose. I thought it would also be good for you to have a handy reference for all those terms here (just in case I missed any). This list isn't exhaustive, and there's no need to read all of them (unless you need help sleeping). Just read the ones you're unfamiliar with.

ANNUAL RECURRING REVENUE (ARR)
Your total revenue (income) from all subscribed customers annualized to one year. This includes all subscription tiers for your products and services, including add-ons and upgrades.

ARR indicates the size and revenue performance of a SaaS business, and buyers want to see that this number has grown every year.

CHURN

Simply put, churn is a measure of the customers lost in a given period. There are several ways you can measure churn, the most common in SaaS being the total number of customers lost against your total remaining for a period of time, expressed as a percentage. But it's not all that simple. How you calculate "lost" and "remaining" customers is up for some debate since you might need to take seasonal customers and the buying characteristics of new customers into account, for example. Nevertheless, you get the basic premise (I hope!).

CUSTOMER ACQUISITION COST (CAC)

The CAC measures how much you spend on acquiring new customers. It includes everything from marketing to sales and equipment to property and is one of the most important metrics for understanding how to grow sustainably.

DEMO-TO-CLOSE RATIO/RATE

This is the number of people who buy your product or service, expressed as a percentage of those to whom you demonstrate your product (what I'd call warm leads). This metric helps indicate how effective your demonstrations are and can highlight problems in sales technique. If this rate is low for your industry, you might need to review closing strategies with your salespeople, for example.

EARNOUT

An earnout is an agreement where you take a lower acquisition price for your business in return for future payments, should the business meet certain financial goals. Usually, you don't want an earnout when selling a business, as you have little influence over what happens when the business changes hands. However, they can be useful to close the gap between the price you want and the price the buyer can or is willing to pay.

EARNINGS BEFORE INTEREST, TAXES, DEPRECIATION, AND AMORTIZATION (EBITDA)

This demonstrates the health of your business. It's one of the key metrics buyers use when determining whether or not to buy your business and at what price.

IDEAL CUSTOMER PROFILE (ICP)

Put simply, this is a detailed analysis and profile of your ideal customer. Think of who your business benefits most and who is worth the most to you. This is your ideal customer, and to correctly market to them, you must first build an ICP. This keeps you focused on the customers that deliver the most value and avoids wasting time and resources on those that don't.

INTELLECTUAL PROPERTY (IP)

Intellectual property refers to intangible property that has been protected via trade secret, patent, or copyright laws. In SaaS, this could refer to software, services, or technology. Whether it's a program you've written or a new technology you've engineered, I recommend you patent or copyright it so no one can steal or reproduce it.

LIEN

A lien is an agreement where you stake property in return for financing or a loan. If you're about to sell a business, ensure you finalize any outstanding liens, as the buyer might not be interested if your assets are currently tied up as collateral for loans. If you can't finalize outstanding liens, at the very least make the buyer aware of them.

LIFETIME VALUE OF CUSTOMER (LTV)

The LTV is an estimate of a customer's entire worth to your company over the course of their time with you. It's a projection of everything the customer might spend on subscriptions, upgrades, add-ons, and other services. It's a useful metric to determine if you're over- or underspending on customer acquisition.

LEAD-TO-MQL/SQL RATIO/RATE

This is the number of customers in your ideal customer bracket (called market-qualified leads, or MQL for short) against the customers who've entered contact information into an online form. When leads become MQLs, you get your salespeople involved, so the higher this rate, the better.

LETTER OF INTENT (LOI)

An LOI is an official expression of interest that a buyer provides a seller. While not legally binding, the LOI is the first "serious" step on the buyer's side and usually signals the start of due diligence and negotiation.

MONTHLY RECURRING REVENUE (MRR)

This is your total revenue (income) from all subscribed customers per month. Like ARR, this includes all subscription tiers for your products and services, including add-ons and upgrades. When you've been going less than a year, or if you want to demonstrate growth on a monthly basis, MRR is ideal and can give insight into the seasonality of your revenue.

MQL/SQL-TO-DEMO RATIO

Market-qualified leads (MQLs) are those that fit your ideal customer profile. The MQL-to-demo ratio is an expression (usually a percentage) of how many of those leads then agree to a product demonstration with a salesperson. The higher this is, the better since it means they're one step closer to buying (should your salespeople close the deal).

NONDISCLOSURE AGREEMENT (NDA)

An NDA is an agreement between you and a third party stating you will not disclose the information shared between you to any other parties. An NDA is common when discussing sensitive details with a potential buyer of your business, for example.

PURCHASE AGREEMENT

The purchase agreement is the final legal agreement that stipulates the transfer of ownership, price to be paid, conditions, and so on of an acquisition. Once your buyer signs this, the company officially belongs to them.

SELLER DISCRETIONARY EARNINGS (SDE)

This is your profit after deducting operating expenses and cost of goods from revenue and then adding in your compensation. SDE is typically used to value small businesses, which is why you add in your compensation. Most small business owners take out compensation from profits, so it's only fair to add it back in when valuing the business.

SELLER FINANCING

Seller financing is when you agree to let a buyer pay you the purchase price for your business in installments. It's a risky measure but increases the size of your buyer pool, as the up-front capital requirements are smaller. Ensure you include a hefty deposit to offset some of the risk.

SOFTWARE AS A SERVICE (SAAS)

SaaS is an industry that developed as a result of our interconnected world. In the past, software companies licensed and installed software on client servers and machines, usually for a one-off cost (subject to costly upgrades).

However, this changed as internet availability and speed increased, enabling a new way of using software that doesn't require localized installation. Instead, customers can access and use their software over the internet.

Free of the restrictions and costs associated with client-side licensing and physical software, SaaS vendors give clients a multi-device, on-demand, pay-as-you-go, instantly scalable mobile software experience.

It's therefore one of the most popular business models in the technology industry.

STOCK SWAP

If you're selling a business to a large, profitable company with a history of doing great things post-acquisition, you might want a slice of that future money pie.

You could, therefore, agree to exchange some or all of your company stock for an equal share in the larger company (or the new entity they'll become after acquisition).

This is called a stock swap and could form part of your acquisition negotiations, assuming you're confident the swap works to your advantage.

VISITOR-TO-LEAD RATIO

This is a measure of how many of the people visiting your website go on to become leads. How you define "lead" depends on your specific business, but it might be when they fill out a contact form, sign up for free (but don't buy anything), or contact you for details about your product, service, or business. Again, the higher this is, the better, as this is the first step toward becoming a customer.

ACKNOWLEDGMENTS

WOW. I WROTE A BOOK. I didn't think this day would ever come—I always assumed I'd be too busy building businesses. Well, what do you know? It happened, and I'd like to thank you, reader, for buying, borrowing, or downloading this book and reading it all the way to the end. I hope you found something useful.

I would like to say an enormous thank you to everyone who's helped, mentored, and supported me over the years. In the spirit of brevity, I won't list everyone here but instead mention a few key figures without whom Bizness Apps simply wouldn't exist.

It starts with my family, whose consistent support, even when times were tough, helped me grow into a positive, tenacious entrepreneur determined to help people succeed. Michelle, thank you for being there when I needed you, for listening to me, for your sacrifices and support while I gave Bizness Apps my life for almost a decade.

Thank you to Christian Friedland and Robert Strazzarino for believing in Bizness Apps and for giving me a shot at turning it into the multimillion-dollar beast it eventually became.

Thank you also to Peter Straus for the inspiration and Tim Porthouse for helping me become a CEO worthy of leadership.

I'd also like to thank Stephen Heisserer, Dave Morton, Rosa Romaine, Brian Cross, Kevin Schrage, and Sam Schnaible for putting your faith in me in the early days and helping turn Bizness Apps into a force of good in the mobile marketing industry.

Finally, I'd like to thank all the people, past and present, who've worked with or under me, whose help inspired me and gave me the confidence to pursue my entrepreneurial dreams. You rock. All of you. And I'm delighted to count you as friends. Entrepreneurship might seem like a solo play, but without you, none of this would've happened.

From the bottom of my heart, thank you.

Made in United States
North Haven, CT
22 June 2022

20481741R00148